WALKING AND TREKKING
IN THE SIERRA NEVADA

WALKING AND TREKKING IN THE SIERRA NEVADA

38 WALKS, SCRAMBLES AND MULTI-DAY TRAVERSES

by Richard Hartley

JUNIPER HOUSE, MURLEY MOSS,
OXENHOLME ROAD, KENDAL, CUMBRIA LA9 7RL
www.cicerone.co.uk

© Richard Hartley 2017
First edition 2017
ISBN: 978 1 85284 917 7
Reprinted 2022 (with updates)

Printed in Singapore by KHL Printing using responsibly sourced paper.
A catalogue record for this book is available from the British Library.
All photographs are by the author unless otherwise stated.

Route mapping by Lovell Johns www.lovelljohns.com
Contains OpenStreetMap.org data © OpenStreetMap
contributors, CC-BY-SA. NASA relief data courtesy of ESRI

Updates to this Guide

While every effort is made by our authors to ensure the accuracy of guidebooks as they go to print, changes can occur during the lifetime of an edition. Any updates that we know of for this guide will be on the Cicerone website (www.cicerone.co.uk/917/updates), so please check before planning your trip. We also advise that you check information about such things as transport, accommodation and shops locally. Even rights of way can be altered over time.

The route maps in this guide are derived from publicly available data, databases and crowd-sourced data. As such they have not been through the detailed checking procedures that would generally be applied to a published map from an official mapping agency, although naturally we have reviewed them closely in the light of local knowledge as part of the preparation of this guide.

We are always grateful for information about any discrepancies between a guidebook and the facts on the ground, sent by email to updates@cicerone.co.uk or by post to Cicerone, Juniper House, Murley Moss, Oxenholme Road, Kendal LA9 7RL, United Kingdom.

Register your book: To sign up to receive free updates, special offers and GPX files where available, register your book at www.cicerone.co.uk.

Front cover: First winter snows on the north faces of Alcazaba and Mulhacén from the Loma de los Cuartos (Route 28)

CONTENTS

Acknowledgements

Mention must be made of the writer of the previous editions of this guide, Andy Walmsley, who published the guide in 1996 with a revision in 2006. These books have spent countless hours accompanying me around the hills of the Sierra Nevada. They also provided much-needed inspiration as I sat around a winter fireside. My sincere hope is that this current guidebook can continue his excellent work.

Walking companions Javier Aguirrebengoa, Nick Cranham, Felipe Nieto Conejero, Clive Fenn, Jens Foell, Victoria Bocanegra Montañes, Andrew Phillips and Ian Tupman provided assistance with photos, route-checking and route choice. Ian Tupman also proofread and highlighted errors in the text.

Local expert Pepe Badaje added information and history about the unguarded refuges. Carol Byrne gave me information about fiesta dates in the Alpujarras. The climate section was checked by weather expert Stephanie Ball of MeteoGib.

The 'Plants and wildlife' section was provided by my wife, Kiersten Rowland, and illustrated with her wonderful photos. She and my daughter, Emma Hartley, also ran the office for long periods whilst I had my head immersed in files and maps. This was invaluable as they removed the few remaining excuses I had to get down to some hard graft.

Thanks to the Hotel España and 'Sabores de las Alpujarras' in Lanjarón for allowing me to use their excellent facilities to spread out the maps, use my laptop, and for keeping me supplied with a seemingly constant stream of coffee or cold beer!

And of course, thanks to Jonathan Williams at Cicerone Press for his guidance, patience and understanding over the years.

Dedicated to my father for introducing me as a 10 year old to the wonders of the hills in the first place.

Morning light illuminating Puntal de la caldera from the Vasar de Mulhacén (Route 8)

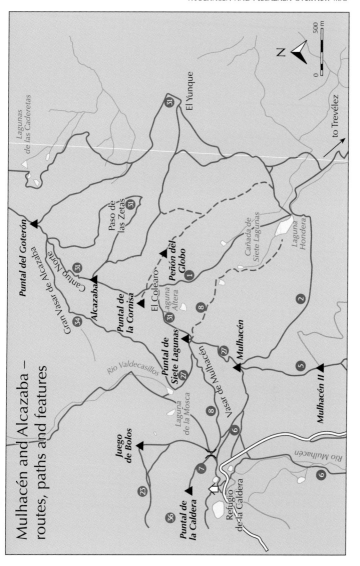

Mulhacén and Alcazaba – routes, paths and features

Lagunas de las Caderetas

Puntal del Goterón

Gran Vasar de Alcazaba

Canuto Norte

Paso de las Zetas

Alcazaba

Puntal de la Cornisa

El Colorado

Peñón del Globo

Laguna del Altera

El Yunque

Cañada de Siete Lagunas

Laguna Hondera

to Trevélez

Puntal de Siete Lagunas

Rio Valdecasillos

Vasar de Mulhacén

Mulhacén

Mulhacén II

Laguna de la Mosca

Juego de Bolos

Rio Mulhacén

Puntal de la Caldera

Refugio de la Caldera

9

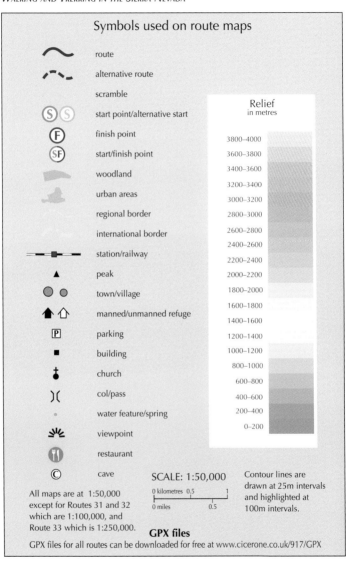

Symbols used on route maps

~	route
⌐ ‑ ‑ ⌐	alternative route
	scramble
Ⓢ Ⓢ	start point/alternative start
Ⓕ	finish point
ⓈⒻ	start/finish point
	woodland
	urban areas
	regional border
	international border
▬■▬	station/railway
▲	peak
● ●	town/village
♠ ⇧	manned/unmanned refuge
P	parking
■	building
♦	church
)(	col/pass
·	water feature/spring
☼	viewpoint
🍴	restaurant
Ⓒ	cave

Relief
in metres

3800–4000
3600–3800
3400–3600
3200–3400
3000–3200
2800–3000
2600–2800
2400–2600
2200–2400
2000–2200
1800–2000
1600–1800
1400–1600
1200–1400
1000–1200
800–1000
600–800
400–600
200–400
0–200

All maps are at 1:50,000 except for Routes 31 and 32 which are 1:100,000, and Route 33 which is 1:250,000.

SCALE: 1:50,000

0 kilometres 0.5   1

0 miles   0.5

Contour lines are drawn at 25m intervals and highlighted at 100m intervals.

GPX files
GPX files for all routes can be downloaded for free at www.cicerone.co.uk/917/GPX

Mountain safety

Every mountain walk has its dangers, and those described in this guidebook are no exception. All who walk or climb in the mountains should recognise this and take responsibility for themselves and their companions along the way. The author and publisher have made every effort to ensure that the information contained in this guide was correct when it went to press, but they cannot accept responsibility for any loss, injury or inconvenience sustained by any person using this book.

International Distress Signal *(emergency only)*
Six blasts on a whistle (and flashes with a torch after dark) spaced evenly for one minute, followed by a minute's pause. Repeat until an answer is received. The response is three signals per minute followed by a minute's pause.

Helicopter Rescue
The following signals are used to communicate with a helicopter:

Help needed:
raise both arms
above head to
form a 'Y'

Help not needed:
raise one arm
above head, extend
other arm downward

Emergency telephone numbers
In case of accident or emergency call 112. Ask for an English speaking operative if you require assistance with the language.

Weather reports
If telephoning from the UK the dialling code is:
Spain: 0034
Teletiempo Sierra Nevada 807 17 03 84
Agencia Estatal de Meteorología 807 17 03 65

Note Mountain rescue can be very expensive – be adequately insured.

ROUTE SUMMARY TABLES

No.	Title	Start	Grade	Distance	Ascent	Time	Page
1	Ascent of Alcazaba via Cañada de Siete Lagunas	Trevélez	Tough	22km	1770m	11hr/2 days	52
2	Ascent of Mulhacén via Cañada de Siete Lagunas	Trevélez	Tough	21km	1870m	11hr/2 days	59
3	Round of the Río Juntillas and Trevélez valleys	Trevélez	Tough or challenging	38km or 35km	2180m or 1670m	2–3 days	64
4	Barranco de Poqueira circular	Capileira	Challenging	20km	930m	8hr	72
5	Ascent of Mulhacén from Hoya del Portillo	Hoya del Portillo	Tough	23.5km	1330m	8hr 30min	76
6	Ascent of Mulhacén from Refugio Poqueira	Refugio Poqueira	Challenging	9.5km	990m	5hr 30min	84
7	The Caldera peaks	Refugio Poqueira	Challenging	10km	680m	6hr	88
8	Around Mulhacén via the Vasar and Siete Lagunas	Refugio Poqueira	Challenging	12km	900m	6hr	91
9	The Púlpitos	Refugio Poqueira	Moderate	10km	670m	4hr 30min	96
10	Pico del Tajo de los Machos and Cerrillo Redondo	Puente Palo	Tough	17.5km	1410m	8hr 30min	103

No.	Title	Start	Grade	Distance	Ascent	Time	Page
11	Ascent of Cerro del Caballo from the south	Trailhead above Lanjarón or Lanjarón	Challenging or tough	19km or 34km	1060m or 2320m	6hr 30min or 13hr 15min/2 days	107
12	Ascent of Cerro del Caballo via Tres Mojones	Mirador de Rinconada	Challenging	11.5km	900m	5hr 15min	112
13	Silleta de Padul	Ermita de las Nieves	Moderate	13km	570m	5hr 30min	117
14	Integral de los Alayos	Merendero los Alayos	Tough	20km	980m	7hr 30min	121
15	Boca de la Pesca	Collado Sevilla	Leisurely	8km	330m	2hr 30min	128
16	Trevenque via Cuerda del Trevenque	Collado Sevilla	Moderate	10km	670m	4hr	130
17	Circuit of Trevenque and Dílar valley	Collado Sevilla	Moderate	12km or 9.5km	900m or 490m	5hr 30min or 4hr 30min	133
18	The Cerro Huenes group	Puente de los Siete Ojos	Moderate	11km	580m	5hr	138
19	Pico del Tesoro and Cerro del Cocón	Casa Forestal Cortijuela	Moderate	8km	350m	3hr 30min	141
20	Trevenque direct	Casa Forestal Cortijuela	Moderate	5km	330m	3hr	145
21	Veleta, Tajos de la Virgen and Lagunillas	Hoya de la Mora	Challenging	17km	850m	7hr	149

13

No.	Title	Start	Grade	Distance	Ascent	Time	Page
22	Veredón Superior and Cerro de los Machos	Hoya de la Mora	Challenging	12.5km	870m	6hr 15min	154
23	Veredón Inferior, Veta Grande, northern flanks and lakes	Hoya de la Mora	Tough	21km	1440m	11hr/2 days	159
24	Across the mountains to Lanjarón	Hoya de la Mora	Tough	29km	860m	11hr/2 days	163
25	Vereda de la Estrella, Refugio Cucaracha and Cueva Secreta	Vereda de la Estrella	Challenging	21km	1250m	8hr	174
26	Cortijos del Hornillo circular	Vereda de la Estrella	Moderate	13.5km	750m	6hr	177
27	Ascent of Mulhacén via Cueva Secreta	Vereda de la Estrella	Very tough	16km	2790m	9hr	180
28	Round of the northern peaks via Peña Partida	Vereda de la Estrella or Loma de los Cuartos	Tough or challenging	37km or 22km	2490m or 1110m	15hr/2–3 days or 10hr 30min/2 days	187
29	Picón de Jérez and round of the Alhorí valley	Refugio Postero Alto	Tough	16km	1330m	8hr	195
30	The eastern peaks	Puerto de la Ragua	Challenging	26km	1510m	2 days	200

Towards Veleta and Cerro de los Machos from the south ridge of Mulhacén (Route 5)

INTRODUCTION

Winter sun setting over the Mediterranean Sea (Route 5)

Tucked away in the south of Spain, in the centre of Andalucía, lies another world. A world of soaring, snow-clad peaks and deep valleys far removed from the crowded beaches of the Costa del Sol. Relatively few foreign visitors to the region venture into the Sierra Nevada – especially in winter, when snow normally lies over the mountains from December until May. It is a very special place.

The Sierra Nevada is not only one of Europe's most southerly mountain ranges, it also contains the highest peaks in Western Europe outside of the Alps. It is a relatively small range of mountains (90km long by 35km wide)

situated in the Granada province of Andalucía, Spain – but what it lacks in size it makes up for in altitude, with over 25 peaks above 3000m. These include the highest point in Western Europe outside the Alps: Mulhacén, at 3482m. From these mountains, on clear days it is possible to view the coast of North Africa some 200km away across the Mediterranean Sea. No glaciers remain here but their effect is marked, with deep cirques and valleys on the northern flanks. By contrast, the southern aspect is relatively gentle.

The range gained national park status in 1999 and covers an area of 85,883 hectares, making it the largest national park in Spain. It was declared a UNESCO Biosphere Reserve in 1986, in recognition of its exceptionally diverse plant, bird and animal species.

The Sierra Nevada is bordered in the west by the plains of the Vega de Granada, while in the east the mountains drop down to merge with the arid desert badlands of Tabernas in Almería. To the north west the hills of the Sierra de Huétor merge into the dry plains around Guadix and Baza to the east; and to the south the Sierra Nevada drops down into the hills of the Alpujarras, a mix of whitewashed villages and lush green valleys fed by the waters of the Sierra Nevada.

The area is very accessible, being only a two-hour drive from the sun-drenched beaches of the Costa del Sol. Despite this it sees relatively few visitors to its slopes, apart from at weekends and during *fiestas* (public holidays) in summer, when the locals enjoy the high mountains. That is, of course, part of the attraction. So close to Africa and the costas and yet so wild and inhospitable. The contrast couldn't be more marked.

There is tremendous scope here for those who prefer their mountains wild and dramatic, as this guidebook will attempt to demonstrate. Yes, it has its trade routes – especially around the easily accessible peaks of Mulhacén (highest) and Veleta (easiest access). Once the decision has been made to venture away from these,

and especially during the week, the area has much to commend it for the seeker of solitude – and especially for multi-day wild camping.

The guide describes routes of varying degrees of difficulty, from easy half-day jaunts and day trips through to tough multi-day treks. Although most are high-level routes in the Sierra Nevada, there are some superb lower-level alternatives that should not be overlooked. These include eight walks in the delightful Cumbres Verdes and Dílar valley hills just south east of Granada. There are also five high mountain scrambles for the more adventurous.

PLANTS AND WILDLIFE

The Sierra Nevada has some of the most exceptional and unique varieties of plant and animal life in the western Mediterranean area. Living conditions are difficult for these species because of the extremes of temperatures and weather.

Plants

Some 116 of the region's 2100 catalogued plants are threatened, and 80 of these are endemic to the Sierra Nevada massif.

Sierra chamomile (*Artemisia granatensis*) is endemic and is on the critical list due to years of being over-collected for its reported healing properties. Another endangered species is the Sierra Nevada poppy (*Papaver lapeyrousianum*), which can

The estrella de las nieves, or 'star of the snows' (Plantago nivalis) (Photo: Kiersten Rowland); the endangered Sierra Nevada poppy (Papaver lapeyrousianum)

only be found in certain areas close to the summit of Mulhacén.

Some of the most fragile and unique ecosystems in the mountain range are the *borreguiles* (high meadows) – home to many of the endemic species, where 35% of the plant species are not found anywhere else in the world. During the spring you'll find a beautiful carpet of alpine flowers and the only carnivorous plant that grows in the Sierra Nevada: the Sierra Nevada Tirana (*Pinguicula nevadensis*), which grows in the wettest areas above 2500m. Depending on snow melt, it blooms in July and catches insects with its sticky leaves.

Probably the most emblematic plant of the Sierra Nevada is the estrella de las nieves ('star of the snows'; *Plantago nivalis*), which has a legend of being the flower of eternal love.

The wide range in altitude here results in two major forest zones: a conifer zone, typical of the higher elevations (1200m–2500m), and a mixed broadleaf zone occuring at mid and lower levels. The park is home to such tree species as Salzmann pine (*Pinus nigra*), Scotch pine (*Pinus sylvestris*), and Maritime pine (*Pinus pinaster*).

Birds

In 2017 it was estimated that over 60 species of bird live in the Sierra Nevada. Birds of prey commonly seen include the golden eagle, Bonelli's eagle, short-toed and booted eagles. Many smaller species such as kestrels, peregrine falcons and goshawks are also frequently spotted.

Griffon vultures are common and seemingly dominate the skies from late spring to autumn. The vulture is nature's natural dustbin-cleaner and does a superb job of clearing the land of unwanted carcasses. The successful reintroduction of the lammergeier (bearded vulture) in a nearby

The colourful bee-eater is found in the lower slopes of the Alpujarras from spring to autumn (Photo: Kiersten Rowland)

mountain range means there's a chance you'll see one of these beautiful rare vultures visiting the Sierra Nevada.

The friendly alpine accentor is found above 2000m and seems to like the Mulhacén summit area in particular in summer. It is mainly resident but winters more widely at lower latitudes.

Skylark, red-billed chough, wheatear and rock thrush are some of the few non-raptors that can be seen, and the ring ouzel visits in winter.

Animals, reptiles and insects
Mammals to be spotted in the Sierra Nevada area include the Spanish ibex (of which there is a thriving population, although it is now facing threats

from illegal hunting and the fatal disease of sarcoptic mange), fox, wildcat, martens, snow vole and wild boar.

Large solitary feline prints have been seen in the snow at 3000m; Lynx are known to frequent the Sierra Arana just north east of Granada, and while it is not inconceivable that they travel south, locals suggest the prints are more likely to be those of a wildcat.

Snakes including the ladder snake, horseshoe whip snake and Lataste's viper can be encountered (see 'General hazards'). Lizards will often be seen sunning themselves on the trails. The ocellated lizard was once traditional cuisine, but is now protected.

There are 270 unique species of insect, with over 100 endemic to these mountains. Most have adapted their life cycles to the extreme conditions; many have become darker, thicker and wingless, such as the endangered saddle bush-cricket.

The Sierra Nevada blue and the Apollo (considered an important

A fine example of a macho Spanish ibex (Cabra Montés) (Photo: Nick Cranham)

Stunning views from Puerto Molina (Route 5)

endemic species), two of the 120 of butterfly species recorded in the region, are also endangered.

CLIMATE AND CONDITIONS

Misjudgment of the weather tends to be due to the changing of the seasons and the related mountain risks that brings. Traditionally, autumn and spring are the most unpredictable times, as it may be t-shirt and shorts weather on the Costa Tropical, yet people could well be fighting blizzard conditions at 3000m. A fine day on the coast can lead unprepared and ill-equipped people into the mountains.

Strangely enough, winter is more predictable. Most mountain-goers recognise the severe weather potential, and that at a bare minimum it will be very cold and windy. The Sierra Nevada does provide some reliable snow cover in the mountains from December to May.

Summer generally offers fine weather for high-level walking and trekking, when it is possible to travel light save for clothing required for the odd afternoon thunderstorm or cooling breezes.

One of the major benefits of the Sierra Nevada is the stability of its climate. Big high-pressure systems sit over the area for months at a time in summer, and sometimes for long periods during the winter months too. The downhill ski resort is said to be the sunniest ski resort in the world. Winter is the most unsettled and wettest period, though, and when bad weather does come in you can expect it to be generally heavy, violent and short-lived.

There are huge differences in temperature between the various seasons. At 3000m in January and February the air temperature (without

High on the west ridge of Trevenque, looking back to the peak of Boca de la Pesca (Route 17)

wind chill) can frequently dip below -10°C. In July and August a normal daytime temperature at 3000m would be 15–20°C. This huge variability – not only between the seasons but also the tremendous altitude differences between the high mountains and the costas – is of course part of the attraction of the place!

Month by month
January and February have many cold, clear and sunny days but there always exists the possibility of some days with heavy snowfalls. Temperatures will be at their lowest in the mountains and so these months tend to provide extensive icing together with short daylight hours. Crampons and

Temperatures (average high/low °C) in Lanjarón (700m), 2009–2016					
Jan	Feb	Mar	Apr	May	Jur
14/5	14/5	16/7	19/10	23/12	27/1

Rainfall (mm/rainy days) in Lanjarón (700m), 2009–2016					
Jan	Feb	Mar	Apr	May	Jur
57/12	59/12	57/12	42/9	23/7	7/3

ice axe, and the ability to use them correctly, are essential.

March and April provide longer days and slightly warmer temperatures. History shows a week of prolonged bad weather during March or April. This late-season snowfall has the advantage of extending the snow and snowshoeing season well into May. Winter hillwalking can be excellent during these months. Crampons and ice axe are essential.

May can provide great snowwalking opportunities, although the snow pack softens markedly after midday. The snows are retreating fast up the mountain now and some routes to 3000m peaks are likely to be clear. There is still some risk of heavy rain showers, lessening towards the end of the month. Some sections of old hard snow will remain at the end of May, possibly necessitating the use of crampons for safe passage. Where such sections exist, notes are given in the route descriptions.

June until end of October provides generally stable mountain conditions. Sunny and warm, this period is especially suited to those looking for hot summer walking under clear blue skies. Walkers can travel light, with water being the heaviest and arguably the most necessary item in the rucksack. It is important to stay protected from the sun's ultraviolet rays and to keep fully hydrated. During these months the heat can give rise to violent but short afternoon storms.

Showers and thunderstorms can move north from Morocco with plumes of very warm air. These, more often than not, are mid-level or high-level showers with bases around 3000m, sometimes below. The thunderstorms are triggered by the topography and movement over the mountains rather than being surface- and convection-based.

The weather phenomenon known as a *gota fría* (the cold drop) can occur in the autumn due to a mix of warm and cold air fronts. It is associated with extremely violent downpours, hail and storms, and can see wind speeds of over 100km/hour. Thankfully these are short-lived and not too common outbursts.

The first major snowfalls can arrive **between the end of October and the end of November**, and further

Jul	Aug	Sep	Oct	Nov	Dec
31/19	30/19	26/16	23/13	17/8	15/6

Jul	Aug	Sep	Oct	Nov	Dec
1/1	2/2	30/6	48/9	71/12	84/13

falls in **December** will generally consolidate the snow pack for the remainder of the winter. In lean years it will be January before this consolidation process has occurred. This period provides very changeable weather and ground conditions: winter one day, spring the next, and back to autumn on day three.

Winter influences

From the west – fronts come in bringing wet weather, falling as snow on high ground above 2000m. This can bring heavy early-season powder, which usually means great news for the skiers but is not so good for road access into the mountains – nor for winter hillwalking, as it may necessitate the use of snowshoes and make things very arduous.

From the north, north east or north west – when these fronts arrive it will be very cold with overnight temperatures between -10°C and -20°C at 3000m. Needless to say the wind chill at these times can be arctic. Snow may fall down to 1000m and very occasionally below this.

From the south – the approach of a southerly front is followed by a quick increase in temperatures, bringing possible rain or a thaw at high altitudes. After the front has passed and the temperatures return to normal, the whole of the Sierra Nevada will become a 'block of ice', leading to potentially very dangerous conditions.

From the east – these fronts are infrequent but wet and give heavy snowfalls, especially to the eastern Sierra Nevada.

The northern and eastern aspect of the Cerro del Caballo, seen from the east (Route 12)

GETTING TO THE SIERRA NEVADA

The Sierra Nevada is very accessible and makes a good destination for last-minute weekend or short breaks as it is close to major airports and fast motorway networks.

Airports

Granada has the closest airport to the range, being only a 1hr drive from the ski area, and is very accessible for the Cumbres Verdes which are on its doorstep. Lanjarón, at the entrance to the Alpujarra, is only 45min away. Capileira, in the heart of the Alpujarra, is 1hr 45min away by car.

At the present time (2017) few airlines go there, besides Iberia/BA and Vueling. The only direct flights from the UK are from London City Airport (British Airways) and from Manchester and London Gatwick (Easyjet). These are not daily flights, though, so you would need to check with the airline direct.

Málaga airport is a 1hr 30min drive away with very easy and fast motorway links to Granada and Lanjarón. There is a huge selection of low-cost daily flights available from most major European departure airports.

Almería provides very easy access to Granada via the A-92 motorway in only 1hr 30min. Fewer flights arrive there than at Málaga, but it is a useful destination if walking in the eastern section of the range.

GETTING AROUND

There is an excellent bus service run by Alsina Graells, based in Granada, between all major towns and villages in the area. Bus travel is cheap but takes longer than a car and has only a limited number of services each day, depending on destination. Check www.alsa.es/en/ for the latest timetables.

Car travel between access points is quick and easy, with fast and relatively traffic-free motorways stretching from near Jérez de Marquesado (A-92 Granada to Almería) to near Lanjarón (A-44 Granada to Motril). The beautiful road through the Alpujarra from Lanjarón to Trevélez (A-4132) is well maintained. Allow an hour between these two towns.

There is no train access around the national park, although Granada links to the major cities of Madrid, Sevilla and Málaga.

Summer ski lift

From late June until the end of August or beginning of September the ski area normally opens a gondola and a chairlift above the ski town of Pradollano. This allows you to travel from the town at 2000m to the cool air of nearly 3000m in 30min. The drop-off point is at the top of the Veleta chairlift, a 15min walk from Posiciones del Veleta. Access to the higher walking trails is very easy from here, but bear in mind that many others will be also treading the trail to Veleta and Mulhacén this way. An

The walking section after the initial buttress on the Espolón de Alcazaba (Route 34)

early start is recommended. Check www.sierranevada.es/en/ for up-to-date opening times and prices. (It's worth noting that the price for a ticket includes the upward and return journey but only for the same day. There are differing price structures if you intend to camp out and come back the following day. Inquire at the ticket office in Pradollano.)

Bus

Autobus Hoya de la Mora 2500m – Posiciones del Veleta 3100m
This service operates from June until mid September – or longer if demand and weather conditions allow. It departs from the Albergue de Granada, just below the Hoya de la Mora above the Pradollano ski station, and drops off just below Posiciones del Veleta. There are numerous daily journeys. It is essential to reserve in advance: tel +34 671 56 44 07.

Autobus Capileira 1436m – Alto de Chorrillo 2700m
This bus departs from the national park information office in Capileira and takes an hour to reach the Alto de Chorrillo at 2700m, making it very convenient for access to day ascents to Mulhacén, Siete Lagunas or Alcazaba. The regular service starts from mid June, but earlier in June and from midway through September until the end of that month there is sometimes a single service morning and evening – although only if enough people have booked (most likely to be on Fridays, Saturdays and Sundays).

Note that in 2017 the national park were trying to scale back this service and its furture remains a long-term doubt. It's absolutely essential that you check times locally and reserve in advance: tel +34 958 763 090 or +34 671 564 406, or email pi.capileira. cma@juntadeandalucia.es

Car hire
Any internet search for car hire at the major airports serving the Sierra Nevada (Granada, Málaga and Almería) will reveal a massive range of vehicles available for hire throughout the year. There are some very enticing and cheap options available – especially during the off-season (winter) months. It's always important, though, to check the small print very

carefully to ensure that you understand what is and what isn't covered within the rental agreement.

It's easy, albeit quite expensive, to hire 4x4 vehicles suitable for dirt and forest tracks. Some of the dirt tracks in this guidebook are suitable for saloon cars (and these are highlighted in the text), but it's very important to make sure your car hire agreement doesn't specifically exclude forest trails and dirt tracks.

Dirt road and four-wheel drive access tracks
Forest roads, dirt roads and off-road tracks are used to access some route start-points, mainly in the south of the range. In winter these are normally passable in 4x4 cars and only at times

Traversing the hillside towards the valley of the Río Seco (Route 9)

when higher snow levels permit. In the summer months, with dry ground, most are passable with care by ordinary saloon cars – especially the track to Hoya del Portillo from Capileira. The worst is usually the Mirador de Rinconada, which often necessitates a 4x4 vehicle.

The routes in question are as follows:

- Route 5 – Hoya del Portillo above Capileira
- Route 10 – Puente Palo for Tajos de los Machos, Cerrillo Redondo
- Route 11 – Peña Caballera, Cerro de Caballo trailhead
- Route 12 – Mirador de Rinconada, Cerro de Caballo trailhead
- Routes 19 and 20 – Casa Forestal de la Cortijuela
- Route 28 – Loma de los Cuartos, Peña Partida (optional)

This is not, however, a definitive subject. As and when local town halls have monetary budget for road reconstruction, the tracks tend to be leveled and cleaned of all potholes, bumps and rocks. On the popular tourist tracks such as access to the Hoya del Portillo above Capileira, this is done annually – normally after the spring rains. Some tracks may have to wait years for money to be spent on them.

Notes are given in the route text where necessary, but it is advisable to ask locally before you arrive. There are some 4x4 services locally that will transport you (for a fee) to or from the trailheads; this is especially useful for some of the end-to-end, linear walks.

For transport to the above routes (and free advice on state of the track), email info@spanishhighs.co.uk; for access from Nigüelas to Mirador de Rinconada (Route 12) in an eight-seater Land Rover, tel +34 696 710 769.

ACCOMMODATION AND BASES

Accommodation in towns and cities

The internet is awash with accommodation choices, from high-quality hotels to budget hostels and camping. There's something to suit all pockets. It is not the intention of this guide to name or recommend hotels, hostels and villas; the best advice is to visit www.booking.com, www.hotels.com or www.tripadvisor.com, where you'll find a wealth of information and reviews to suit every budget and requirement.

In the following area summaries, timings indicate length of journey by car.

Granada area

Granada is extremely convenient for the Cumbres Verdes and Dílar valley routes (20min; Routes 13–20), the ski area/Hoya de la Mora (30min; Routes 21–24) and the Vereda de Estrella trailhead (40min; Routes 25–28). Some hotels alongside the main ski road to the Sierra Nevada provide good and higher alternatives to the city if you intend to do some walks from this side.

Looking back from the main summit of Boca de la Pesca to the second summit and ascent route (Route 15)

The Alpujarras

This area is very close to the southern approaches and trailheads into the range, and there is a good range of hotel, apartment and villa accommodation in most towns and villages.

The town of Lanjarón – *Puerta de la Alpujarra* ('Door to the Alpujarra') – is just 10min from the main A-44 Granada to Motril motorway, and is useful for the Cerro del Caballo (Routes 11 and 12) and access to Puente Palo (Route 10). It is also a spa town, so plenty of treatments are available to soothe your aching limbs after completing the Tres Miles Integral (Route 31)! Órgiva is a further 15min drive away.

You need to travel further into the Alpujarras if you prefer smaller towns and villages and/or wish to get closer to the majority of the routes in this guide that start from the south. The three 'white villages' of the Poqueira gorge – Pampaneira, Bubión and Capileira – cling to the hillsides below Mulhacén and provide close access to plenty of routes. Allow an hour for the journey to these villages from the A-44 Granada to Motril motorway exit for Lanjarón.

Trevélez is a further 20min along the road, passing through Pitres, Pórtugos and Busquístar. Below the road, the delightful and sleepy villages in the Taha de Pitres, consisting of Mecina, Fondales and Ferrierola, can provide a very relaxing place to rest after the rigours of the mountains. Trevélez itself is a substantial tourist town and has good accommodation options. Trevélez is a start-point for ascents to Siete Lagunas, Mulhacén, Alcazaba and excursions up the Río Trevélez.

Bear in mind that this is still a very traditional area so most towns will have at least one major annual fiesta during the year. At fiesta time accommodation will be difficult if not impossible to find so should be booked well in advance.

Many hotels in the Alpujarras shut down for winter and can be closed from the end of autumn until just before Easter. Some will just close for January and others will close for Christmas and New Year, when family becomes more important than paying guests. Bear this in mind when planning a winter visit.

Jérez del Marquesado

There's not too much in the way of accommodation in Jerez del Marquesado – just a couple of hostels – but the major town of Guadix is just 30min up the motorway towards Granada.

Campsites

Most towns in the region have official campsites nearby. These have organised facilities and are somewhat 'luxurious'. Not all are open year-round so it's advisable to check locally. (See Appendix B.) In addition, tents can become rather too hot for comfort in the long hot summers – and conversely, very cold in the winter months when valley temperatures can drop below freezing.

NOTABLE FIESTAS

- **Trevélez** – Fiesta of San Antonio (13 and 14 June); Saint Benedict (11 July); Mulhacén pilgrimage to the Virgen de las Nieves (5 August); cattle show (19 and 20 October).

- **Capileira** – Fiesta de la Virgen de la Cabeza (last Sunday in April); also a second fiesta for the same saint during the second week in August; *romería* (pilgrimage) to Mulhacén (5 August); Fiesta de la Castaña (beginning of November).

- **Órgiva** – San Sebastian (20 January); procession on Maundy Thursday; Fería Hecho en la Alpujarra (Holy Week); Fiesta Virgen de la Fe (14 June); Fería Grande (end of September).

- **Lanjarón** – Fiesta de San Juan (around 21–25 June) – carnivals, processions and the world's biggest water fight!

Guarded refuges

There are three guarded refuges in the range: Refugio Poqueira, which is open all year, Refugio Postero Alto whose opening depends on the season, and Refugio Albergue Universitario de Granada, open all year. See Appendix B for further details.

Reciprocal rights at the guarded refuges

Major alpine clubs have reciprocal rights for reduced overnight and meal fees. These include the Federación Andaluza de Montanismo, Austrian Alpine Club, Deutscher Alpenverein, Club Alpin Français, Italian Alpine Club and Club Alpin Swiss. A full list can be found on the Refugio Poqueira website: www.refugiopoqueira.com

The affiliations normally run for a calendar year and are very good value. On showing your affiliated card, the price of a night's accommodation at the Refugio Poqueira hut is substantially reduced. Note that the British Mountaineering Council (BMC) does not have reciprocal rights with Andalucian refuges.

Refugio de Poqueira
(Routes 6, 7, 8, 9, 32)

An excellent guarded refuge with 85 beds open all year and an excellent meal service, it lies on a small plateau at 2500m just south east of the Río Mulhacén. It is affiliated to the Federación Andaluza de Montañismo and has reciprocal rights with the major European alpine clubs. It's essential to reserve well in advance.

Normal winter access is recommended from Capileira (Cebadilla Eléctrica) and via the more sheltered Barranco de Poqueira. Early or late season access in calm conditions can also be made from the *acequias*

Refugio Poqueira in the depths of winter

(irrigation channel) route or from the Hoya del Portillo.

The Refugio Poqueira website (www.refugiopoqueira.com) gives a very useful weekly report on the status of the unguarded refugios Vivac La Caldera and Villavientos, along with important information about the current snow and mountain conditions.

Refugio Postero Alto (Routes 29, 31)
This refuge makes a very convenient start-point and is ideally placed to access the first northerly 3000m+ peaks of the Sierra Nevada. It lies at the foot of the Picón de Jérez at 1900m and is good for accessing

Barranco del Alhorí, the northern Sierra Nevada, and indeed the 'Los Tres Miles' Integral (Route 31).

The refuge is open at weekends and during fiesta holidays (Easter, Christmas, New Year); otherwise there's a winter quarters that is always open and available. Facilities include a canteen, bar, hot water plus heating in all rooms. Sleeps 64.

It's affiliated to the Federación Andaluza de Montañismo, which has reciprocal rights with the major European alpine clubs (see above). Reservation in advance is essential and can be done online at www. refugioposteroalto.es/reservar/

Refugio Elorrieta; Refugio Peña Partida; Refugio Cucaracha
(Photo: Victoria Bocanegra Montañes); Refugio Cebollar

A useful service offering transfers from Jérez del Marquesado to the refuge in 4WD vehicles has recently started: www.refugioposteroalto.es/traslados-en-4x4/

Albergue Universitario de Granada

This refuge is situated at 2500m close to the Hoya de la Mora above the ski area. It can be reached by saloon car and is a convenient point for access, especially in winter, to the Veleta area. The capacity of the hostel is 59 places in either double rooms or dormitories with bunk beds. Showers, dining room service, bar-cafeteria, TV room and central heating. Website alberguesierranevada.com

Unguarded refuges

These are simple shelters and sleeping arrangements are basic. They are possibly most useful in the winter months when carrying the extra weight of winter equipment. The more modern and populated ones have elevated wooden boards to sleep on, and at worst you'll have to sleep on a concrete floor. Take an insulated sleeping mat and sleeping bag, along with a stove, food and fuel. Nearby water sources are indicated below, but in winter months snow for melting is usually close to hand. Make sure you overestimate the amount of fuel required to melt snow.

There is no booking system in place for these refuges: they operate on a first come, first served basis. Bear this in mind on Friday and Saturday evenings throughout the year, when the popular refuges (Carihuela, Caldera, Refugio Forestal de Loma Pela and Caballo) will get busy with locals. On these nights you can expect late arrivals, with locals having finished work earlier in the day. Try to remain calm as they chat, eat, drink and snore their way through the night. Some good ear plugs are advised!

Many of the unguarded refuges hold a lot of history, dating back to Franco's early days and a plan to reforest the Sierra Nevada. There are actually many more refuges hidden away, but many of these are uninhabitable or in complete ruin.

The refuges below are listed in the order that they appear in this guide. For grid references and additional details, see Appendix B.

Refugio Horcajo (Route 3)

Situated at 2220m, 3hr from Trevélez above the Río Trevélez junction with the Río Juntillas and Río Puerto de Jérez. Sleeps 8 on concrete floors. The refuge is in a reasonable state, with water available close by from Barranco del Sabinar.

Refugio Vivac La Caldera (Routes 6, 7, 8, 23, 31, 35, 36)

Located at 3100m just east of Laguna de la Caldera, west of Mulhacén, this refuge is useful for access to Mulhacén, Alcazaba and Puntal de la Caldera. Sleeps 16. It's in a good state with wooden boards for sleeping on. Water can be accessed at the lake of the same name just west of the refuge.

**Refugio Forestal Loma Pela
(also known as Refugio Villavientos)**
On the south side of Loma Pelada, at an altitude of 3090m, this is useful for access to Mulhacén, Alcazaba and Puntal de la Caldera. The refuge is in a very good state and makes a convenient alternative to Refugio Caldera on busy weekends. Sleeps 8. The only downside is that there is no water source close by, so all water must be carried in.

**Refugio Forestal Loma de Cañar
(Cebollar) (Route 10)**
Situated at 2500m on a beautiful alpine meadow, this refuge has its own spring close by that never seems to dry up. It's worth a visit and an overnight stay if possible. The refuge itself is a bit rough but reasonably comfortable – although the roof does leak a bit. Sleeps 10. Good for an ascent of Tajos de los Machos or a winter outing thereabouts.

Refugio de Ventura (Routes 11, 24, 31)
At the top edge of the forest by the path descending from Cerro del Caballo, the building is partially ruined and should only be used in an emergency, as it's only an hour to a road trailhead or a 3hr walk down to Lanjarón. There is no convenient water source.

**Refugio del Caballo
(Routes 11, 24, 31)**
This one-room bivouac hut takes the form of a small, semi-cylindrical domed shelter and is located at an altitude of 2860m next to the Laguna del Caballo at the base of the north east face of Cerro del Caballo. Sleeps 8. In the summer of 2011 the 'Acción Sierra Nevada' initiative (www. accionsierranevada.org) installed a door, painted the inside, put in a window and cleaned the refuge from top to bottom. Work to the roof in 2014 has improved it as a suitable winter shelter. The lake a few metres west meets all water requirements.

Refugio Elorrieta (Routes 21, 24, 31)
The Elorrieta Refuge is located at 3197m, south west of the Tajos de la Virgen ridge. It was built between 1931 and 1933 and named in honour of the Director General Octavio Elorrieta. It was the most ambitious of a network of shelters created in the 1930s in the Lanjarón river valley. It

NATURAL SHELTERS

There are natural shelters and caves at:

- Cueva Secreta, 1780m, lower Valdeinfiernos valley, Genil (grid reference 708 050)

- Refugio 'Natural' Siete Lagunas, 2870m, next to Laguna Hondera where there are natural shelters and walls (grid reference 739 001). A shovel may be required in winter.

originally had central heating, water, and power for lighting. It consists of two parts: a domed outside shelter and another series of galleries and tunnels dug out of the rock. However, the annual seasonal temperature extremes have taken their toll, and the roof is in particularly bad shape. Time and vandalism have done the rest. It was partially rebuilt in the 1960s but is now once again in a dismal state. It can nevertheless be useful for shelter from inclement weather.

Refugio Vivac La Carihuela (Routes 22, 23, 31, 32)

Situated at 3200m on the col (Collado de Carihuela) south of Veleta, this refuge is in a very good state with wooden bunks and a table. Sleeps 16. It's especially useful in winter or during a summer traverse of Los Tres Miles. In early summer water may be found by dropping down the road to the east to melting snow streams dripping from rocks; in late summer an excursion to Laguna de Aguas Verdes may have to be undertaken.

Refugio Forestal La Cucaracha (Routes 25, 28)

Located at 1800m on the Cuesta del Calvario above the Río Genil, and given a makeover in 2014, this part-ruin provides adequate winter shelter and is useful for ski touring on the northern peaks. Sleeps 15–20. Access is from Güéjar Sierra and Vereda de Estrella. Water can be found at Fuente de los Lirios (10min south west down towards the river from the refuge – but remember there's a 15–20min climb back!).

Refugio Peña Partida (Route 28)

This refuge lies at 2451m on the eastern shoulder of Loma de los Cuartos above the town of Güéjar Sierra. High snow level or a 4WD car is required to access Loma de los Cuartos to a car parking space with a chain across the track. It's a 2hr walk from here. The refuge is in a good state of repair, with magnificent views to the northern faces of the Sierra Nevada. Wooden sleeping platforms were installed as part of a 2015 restoration. Sleeps 10; water can be found at a small natural spring 300m south east of the refuge at the upper end of Barranco de Peña Partida.

RESPECTING THE ENVIRONMENT

The Sierra Nevada gained national park status in 1999. Most of the zone to which this guide relates is within the national park boundaries. It is a very special place and it is therefore important that visitors treat it with great respect.

- You do not need to obtain authorisation for climbing and mountaineering in the high mountains.
- You do not need permission to use the unguarded refuges, but please take all litter away with you, leave the place in as clean

Spectacular lenticular clouds over Mulhacén (Route 21)

a state as possible and **close the door and windows** so that snow does not enter.

It goes without saying that you should not:

- make fires
- feed the wildlife
- disturb the tranquility of nature
- go hunting or fishing
- leave any type of discharge in water sources, rivers or lakes
- allow dogs off-leash
- collect plants, minerals or rocks.

Remember that the 'borreguiles' (high meadows) are a highly sensitive environment; shelters and walls for a bivouac should be made well outside the green lakeside locations as they can cause irreparable damage to the unique flora and fauna of these places.

The Sierra Nevada National Park authority can be contaced at Ctra. Antigua de Sierra Nevada, Km 7, 18191 Pinos Genil, tel +34 958 026300, email pn.snevada.cma@ juntadeandalucia.es

SAFETY AND RESCUE

The following points are intended as reminders for staying safe in the mountains.

Check the weather forecast: consult online weather resources such as AEMET (www.aemet.es/en/) and the Sierra Nevada ski pages (www. sierranevada.es/en/), looking out for wind gust speeds at your intended altitude. Temperatures both the night before and on the day of your climb will indicate likely ground conditions

NATIONAL PARK CAMPING GUIDELINES

Camping is allowed in the national park but there are rules and restrictions. An overnight bivouac is permitted using a bivouac bag or lightweight tent. The following rules apply to small groups of three or fewer tents (max 15 persons); larger groups should apply to the national park authority (see above). You should notify the national park office of your intention to camp by post or email.

• You can only set up a tent one hour before sunset and it must be taken down within one hour of sunrise.

• You can only stay one night in the same place.

• You can only camp above 1600m. In summer this rises to above the tree line (about 2200m) due to fire risk.

• Leave no trace and take all rubbish out with you.

You must not camp:

• within 500m of a guarded refuge or public vehicle track

• within 1km of a tarmac road

• within 50m of a mountain lake or river

• on private property without written permission from the owner.

(ice, soft snow etc) and also the likely wind chill factor.

Dress accordingly: take spare clothing – the extra weight will be well worth it when the clouds come in and winds increase. In winter, pack a down jacket and extra gloves, even on the best of days.

Take a fully charged mobile phone with you: this is absolutely essential in case you get into difficulty and need the rescue services. Remember that cold affects battery life/performance – consider carrying a spare battery.

Dial 112 to contact the emergency services. There is good coverage around the ski area, variable coverage on the major summits and elsewhere. In sheltered northern valleys there will be none. Remember that even if your mobile is showing zero or little signal strength, it may be possible to connect to emergency services via 112. The Delorme InReach satellite text system is useful in these mountains as a form of communication when mobile phone service doesn't exist.

Don't bite off more than you can chew! Your intended route should be well within your capability and experience – especially in winter above the snow line. Be prepared to change

Approaching Collado de Vacares, with Alcazaba behind (Route 28)

your plan as mountain conditions change; familiarise yourself with the quickest escape route and the location of refuges/shelters that could be utilised if required.

Take a map and compass: standalone GPS devices can be very useful, but don't rely on a smartphone GPS as battery capability will be limited in very cold temperatures. Always carry a sheet map and compass.

Take crampons and ice axe: if you're heading above the snow line, crampons and ice axe (and the ability to use them) are essential. There are plenty of basic winter skills courses in the Sierra Nevada and the UK that will give you sufficient training and confidence to take modest steps into the

mountains during winter. See www. spanishhighs.co.uk for details.

Inform people of your route: make sure you tell somebody your intended route and what time you intend to be back.

Assess the risk of avalanche: check with the Sierra Nevada ski area (www. sierranevada.es/en/) and/or Refugio Poqueira (www.refugiopoqueira.com). See also 'Winter hazards', below.

'The mountains will always be there, the trick is to make sure you are too.'
Hervey Voge

'Mountains have a way of dealing with over-confidence.'
Herman Buhl

General hazards

Underestimating the Sierra Nevada

In benign summer mode with its hot sun, clear skies, easy access and closeness to the fleshpots of the Costa del Sol, it's easy to underestimate the scale of the Sierra Nevada; but these are high mountains, and distances both in vertical metres and horizontal kilometres are great. Take away the easy access and settled, stable weather and it's a long way home! Many underestimate these hills each year, thus adding to the accident statistics. The Sierra Nevada needs to be treated with the utmost respect.

Falling

Common-sense precautions against falls – both of humans and of rocks from above – should be taken on all routes. In addition, helmet, harness and rope are advised for security on all of the high mountain scrambles – with the possible exception of Route 21 (Tajos de la Virgen ridge), where there are only a couple of simple scrambling sections and no danger of rockfall. A helmet would also be advisable on Route 8 (Vasar de Mulhacén) to protect from any falling rocks.

Dehydration

Here more than anywhere it is vital to keep hydrated. The intense sun and high altitudes combine to suck water out of the body. In summer make sure you carry a minimum of three litres of water, and make sure you drink on a regular basis.

Altitude

These mountains have much high ground over 3000m. That and the fact that is is possible to ascend 2000m in a car in 30 mins mean that the effects of altitude can be felt. However, they are generally quite mild with shortness of breath and perhaps a slight headache. As always, the general advice is to go slow, especially on leaving the high car parks. Within an hour breathing should have eased and the body adjusted somewhat.

The sun

At all times of the year, sun and lip cream are necessary. In the summer months a sun hat covering the back of the neck is recommended. Many people prefer to walk the high hills in summer wearing t-shirt and shorts; due to the prickly nature of the vegetation, the sharp loose rock and the risk of sunburn to uncovered parts of the body, it is advisable to cover up with long trousers and sleeves.

Foxes

Spanish foxes – at least in the Sierra Nevada – are not like English solitary foxes as they have been known to work in groups. If you're camping out, they will come at night to take your food, putting their heads under the side of your tent to grab anything they can find, especially if you keep items in plastic bags. If it's not food, it will

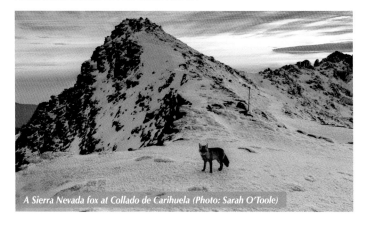

A Sierra Nevada fox at Collado de Carihuela (Photo: Sarah O'Toole)

be discarded nearby. If it is, you won't see it again.

They are a particular problem at the more utilised camping and bivouac sites, even in the depths of mid-winter. Siete Lagunas, Laguna del Caballo, around the vicinity of Refugio Carihuela and at Laguna de la Caldera seem to be the worst locations, but they have also been encountered at Collado de Vacares and Laguna de Juntillas in the far north of the range.

In the summer months the presence of a dog will deter, but this is often not possible for those on a walking or hiking holiday. Another option is to use an anti-fox beacon: this innovative and humane deterrent detects body heat, and once triggered it releases bursts of ultrasound, resulting in the fox retreating. FOXWatch (www.conceptresearch.co.uk) produce one. Otherwise, unless you stay in a fox-proof hut, you have to accept fox raids as a possible natural part of mountain life in the Sierra Nevada.

Don't try zipping up your tent to keep them out; they will just claw their way in and leave your tent in tatters. Let them come in and see there's nothing to take. Tie your pack to yourself so they can't pull it out of the tent. Better still, bury food outside under rocks and put boots inside your rucksack. Accept that you will be woken up and don't let it worry you; they're unlikely to hurt you. Be grateful you're not camping in bear country! If you're careful, you won't lose anything of value.

Snakes

There are two main poisonous snakes in the region. Lataste's viper is usually found between 800m and 2800m; adults are normally less than 60cm in length and have a snub nose. The Montpellier snake can be found anywhere up to 2150m altitude and can grow to 240cm/3kg. Its teeth are set at the back of its top jaw, so you would have to be manhandling the snake in order to be bitten. Like most snakes, both of these species will be more eager to get away from you than vice versa – provided you give them a wide berth and treat them with respect. However, their bites are not considered serious for most healthy people.

Pine processionary caterpillars

These harmless-looking caterpillars (which turn into moths) can be very dangerous to humans and pets. When disturbed, the caterpillars shed their fine harpoon-shaped hairs, which cause itchy rashes and breathing problems. (Just sitting under a tree that contains a nest can cause a rash.) Some people can have severe allergic reactions.

The caterpillars are a big problem in Spain's pine forests. It was once thought that they killed trees, but studies have shown they do not attack a tree after it has been weakened; they leave it to recover and start again once it's strong enough. Danger time is normally in the spring but can be earlier in mild winters, when the caterpillars leave their nests to find suitable ground to pupate.

Electrical storms

These are a common occurrence in late spring and autumn but are rare in winter. Sufficient warning is usually posted on the AEMET website (www. aemet.es/en/).

Wildfires

Andalucía has a very high incidence of forest wildfires, especially between the beginning of May and the end of October. One particularly large wildfire in 2005 above Lanjarón destroyed over 8000 hectares of the National Park. Please exercise the utmost caution, even outside of these high risk dates.

Winter hazards

Avalanches

Most winters and after fresh snowfall there are avalanches all over the Sierra Nevada, but they are normally small and localised. An exception was in February 2011 when a massive slide nearly 1km wide killed one person and injured two others in Barranco de San Juan.

There are four major black spots that regularly avalanche and have become scenes of accidents because they cross normal walking or hiking trails:

- north west of the Tajos de la Virgen ridgeline on the track between Lagunillas de la Virgin and Refugio de Elorrieta (Routes 21, 24). This path crosses steep and dangerous avalanche terrain, and its proximity to the ski centre means increased human traffic. For experienced mountaineers the ridge of the Tajos de la

Virgen is safer; or the whole can be avoided by an easy, safe but longer snow ascent up the Tozal de Cartujo via the bowl west of the north west ridge of Cartujo.

- Paso de los Franceses on the south west slopes of Mulhacén above the normal walking track up the Río Mulhacén (Route 5). In particular the old road above this area can be very dangerous. Give this a wide berth westwards on the approach to the west flank route of Mulhacén or the Col de Ciervo. In 1989 an accident here cost the lives of six French mountaineers.

- Paso de los Machos on the south side of Cerro de Los Machos where the old road cuts through a small pass (Routes 23, 31, 32). This area is normally heavily loaded with snow in winter, and the path is used as a quick and easy approach from Carihuela to Mulhacén or the Poqueira/Caldera areas. If heading for Refugio Poqueira, a safer descent is via Loma Pua, Pico de Sabinar and cut through the Terreras Azules below Pico del Púlpito.

- Barranco de San Juan (Route 23), whose proximity to Hoya de la Mora and low altitude increase the risk to mountain-goers. It's usually full of wind-blown snow after major snowfalls; there are lots of small localised dangers but a massive avalanche in February 2011 has increased awareness of the potential for large-scale slides

here. The main route up Veleta (Route 21) totally avoids the valley. It goes without saying that good mountaineering and avalanche awareness practices should be observed on all routes in the high mountains. There's a useful online tutorial at www.avalanche.org; and 'Be Avalanche Aware', run by the Scottish Avalanche Information Service, provides a good online resource at www.beaware.sais.gov.uk. However, the above blackspots should always be avoided or bypassed.

Icing

After a southerly front from the African continent passes northwards through the Sierra Nevada there is a rapid rise in temperature followed by a quick return to sub-zero. This turns the Sierra Nevada into a gigantic block of ice where a slip by the tired or inexperienced can have disastrous consequences. In winter 2014 many experienced mountaineers got into difficulties on simple routes and had to resort to assistance from the rescue services.

Sharp crampons and ice axes are essential – along with knowledge of how to use them! Choosing a simpler or less exposed route will lessen the risk.

Winds

Predominantly from the west, these are a constant companion in the high mountains. It's not uncommon for gusts of over 100km/hr to be recorded in winter – and indeed a winter gust of

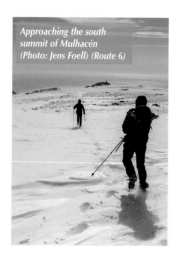
Approaching the south summit of Mulhacén (Photo: Jens Foell) (Route 6)

over 200km/hr was once recorded at an altitude of 2800m.

Progress will be difficult and may well be impossible in winds of over 60km/hr, especially on ridges and in areas where the wind is funneled through passes such as Collado de Carihuela. In addition, when strong, bitterly cold winds arrive from the north the wind chill will be extremely high.

Blizzards

A combination of snow and high winds can turn a relatively gentle outing on an accessible mountain into a life-and-death struggle. It's important to remember and respect the high altitudes and the sometimes long distances involved in reaching safety. Local mountaineers don't leave home in these conditions, but if you do happen to get caught out it will

help if you've done your homework with regard to map, compass, escape routes etc. However, given today's wealth of online weather resources, such problems should not occur.

Snow bridge collapse

This happens in the spring melt when rivers and streams carve tunnels beneath the valley snows. The unstable snows above look perfectly fine to walk on but can collapse, causing injury.

WATER SOURCES

In the spring, rivers and streams gush down the hillsides of the Sierra Nevada, swollen by the snowmelt waters, and there is no problem locating suitable drinking water. In fact water is not an issue until July, when these streams start to dry up and eventually disappear (although after ample snow years some patches of hard snow may remain throughout the summer on north-facing slopes, especially in the Corral del Veleta and on Mulhacén and Alcazaba). In late August, September and until the rains arrive, walkers may have to rely on the lakes for water, taking water from the lake itself if there is no flowing exit stream. The waters of the Sierra Nevada are normally very pure, but the best advice is to use a filter to remove any protozoa, bacteria or cryptosporidium.

An indication as to the location of water sources is given where necessary in individual route descriptions in this guide.

Conoce Tus Fuentes (Know Your Springs) is a good online resource that lists and maps all the springs and water sources in Andalucia (in Spanish): www.conocetusfuentes.com

There are many online weather resources available for the Sierra Nevada. The following have been found to be useful in terms of both current and future weather influences.

Spanish Met Office (AEMET)

Specific mountain weather forecasts can be found at www.aemet.es/en/ (from the main menu, select Weather > Forecast > Mountains). Weather Alerts are available from the same site and are also available on the AEMET weather app for iOS and Android.

Others

The Sierra Nevada ski website (www. sierranevada.es/en/) is specifically designed for the ski area but their forecasts and webcams give a good indication of what can be expected in the mountains as a whole.

The Instituto de Astrofísica de Andalucía has a weather station (Observatario Sierra Nevada, 2880m) that is useful for determining current conditions and trends: www.osn.iaa. es/meteo.

Meteo Exploration mountain forecasts can be found at www.meteoexploration.com. Enter your required mountain summit into

Tajos Altos from the path traversing east of the summit of Cerro del Caballo (Route 12)

the search field. They have various locations in their database, including El Caballo (Cerro del Caballo), Veleta, Mulhacén, Picón de Jérez and Trevenque, as well as Refugio Poqueira and Refugio Postero Alto.

PLANNING AND MAPS

Don't expect the same level of accuracy in Spanish mapping that exists, for example, in the UK with Ordnance Survey maps. There are a variety of maps available that are relatively accurate, although you should be on the lookout for possible errors – especially with regard to dirt access roads. In addition, the names and altitudes of some peaks differ across the various maps.

The recommended and most accurate maps are listed below. In this guide, altitudes and nomenclature are standardised as per the Editorial Penibética maps.

- Parque Nacional de Sierra Nevada 1:40,000 (Editorial Penibética)
- Sierra Nevada – La Integral de los 3000m 1:25,000 (Editorial Piolet)

These can be bought from most major retailers such as Stanfords (www.stanfords.co.uk). The Penebética map is also available from www.articodis.com

Open Cycle Map

With the onset of mobile apps to help navigate your way around the world, the standard and accuracy of digital mapping has improved in recent years. Mention must be made of the open source mapping software Open Cycle Map (www.opencyclemap.org) – an online global map based on data from the OpenStreetMap project. This can be a useful resource to download and use on your phone, tablet, computer or indeed GPS.

USING THIS GUIDE

Routes are grouped according to access point, starting from the south east in Trevélez in the Alpujarras and travelling clockwise around to the north east at Jérez del Marquesado. One route begins in the far east at the Puerto de la Ragua (Route 30). A variety of the best walks or multiday treks from each access point is offered.

Some walks necessarily overlap, and this affords the opportunity to extend or 'bolt on' an additional section to suit. There are countless possible variations throughout the Sierra Nevada; it is the sincere hope that this guide explains the best of the possibilities and provides an inspiration for the reader to go out and explore others.

Times

Timings include normal short refreshment breaks and camera halts etc along the route, but they exclude extended stops. They allow for a slower rate of travel at altitude. They are calculated for summer ascents only; ascents in winter may take longer

45

due to additional rucksack weight and variations in conditions underfoot.

The times are based on those of a reasonably fit person in their early 60s (the author) and happen to equate closely to Naismith's rule. Adjust timings accordingly if you are younger and fitter – or maybe even older than the author! (Naismith's rule was devised by William W Naismith, a Scottish mountaineer, in 1892. The basic rule has been adjusted over time, and it states that you should allow 1hr for every 4km forward, plus 1hr for every 600m of ascent and 45min for every 500m of descent.)

For the scambles, the time given in the information box reflects scrambling time only; approach time is provided separately.

Seasonal notes

Due to the large variation in climate and mountain conditions during the year, the routes are accompanied by seasonal notes where relevant. These include potentially difficult or dangerous sections for the winter hill walker, as well as the location of suitable water sources during the long, hot summer months.

Route descriptions

Unless otherwise stated, the route descriptions assume summer conditions. That is, that there is no snow affecting the route, and that there are high temperatures with light winds and clear visibility. Allowance should be made accordingly for any bad weather or winter conditions.

Information board at the mirador near the start of the route, with Trevenque prominent ahead and the snow-covered Sierra Nevada beyond (Route 16)

It is assumed that the reader has a good level of navigational and map reading competence – thus not every twist and turn of the path is described; just the major points of navigational and directional importance. However, in the route description, places or features along the way that are highlighted in **bold** correlate with those shown on the route map, to aid navigation.

Intermediate timings and distances are provided throughout the route descriptions; unless otherwise stated, these measure from the start of the main route.

Walking and scrambling grades

The grading of walks is subjective but the following grades have been applied in an attempt to convey the character and overall difficulty of a walk to the reader. It should be noted that use of summer ski lifts or the park bus services to gain altitude will reduce the difficulty and given grade.

Leisurely

No experience necessary. Anyone fit and healthy enough to complete a weekend walk should be able to manage these. Short walks (usually of 3–5 hours' duration) on good, well-maintained paths or tracks at low altitude. No navigational difficulties.

Moderate

Those with hill-walking experience should be able to manage these routes. Good health and reasonable fitness required as there are some longer/harder days (with an average of 5–7 hours' duration). Usually no extremes of altitude or ascent/decent and walking generally on good paths, but with some rocky terrain. Navigation fairly straightforward.

Challenging

Fitness is important on these routes and you may have to improve it before departure. Most treks involve extended walking in mountainous terrain, usually at significantly higher altitudes. Climate and remoteness can also play a part. Previous trekking experience is therefore desirable. Six to eight hours per day with occasional longer days on peaks or passes. Treks may include difficult terrain (including loose scree), high altitudes, occasional significant daily ascents and overnights in remote areas. Potential navigation difficulties in poor weather.

Tough

Tough treks in remote mountain landscapes, so stamina essential as walking days are long and hard. It is recommended that you have previous trekking experience – preferably at altitude – as well as complete confidence in your physical condition and self-reliance. Treks may involve difficult terrain (possibly with some scrambling sections), extremes of altitude and significant ascent/decent (a number of days feature over 1000m of ascent). Navigation difficult in poor conditions. Remote, wild environments with few facilities, perhaps for

Looking back along the Vasar de Mulhacén to Veleta (Route 8)

extended periods – be prepared to rough it!

Very tough

Treks include all the elements of the previous grade, but with extra difficulties such as tricky river crossings, very high or difficult passes, navigational problems or peaks that require basic climbing skills.

Scrambling grades

A final section in this guide highlights five fine high-mountain scrambles from Grade 2 to Grade 3S for those who are looking for a bit more of an adrenaline rush. The selection given here merely scratches the surface of

the possibilities in the region, however; there's plenty of scope for future development!

- **Grade 1** – no specialist mountaineering skills required. Technically easy although a head for heights may be required at times
- **Grade 2** – more serious, possibly needing some simple technical skills. Rope and safety gear should be used
- **Grade 3** – similar to Grade 2 but with simple pitches of easy rock climbing. More technical rope work and protection required
- **Grade 3(S)** – serious. Some short sections of moderate/difficult rock climbing may be encountered.

WALKS

Descending the south ridge of Cerro del Caballo with superb views towards the Sierra de Almijara and the Mediterranean Sea (Route 11)

TREVÉLEZ

Crossing the streams that mark the entrance to the Cañada de Siete Lagunas (Route 1)

The popular village of Trevélez (1476m) is reputed to be the highest in Spain, although it is more famous for its fine and tasty selection of hams – and is perhaps best known for its mouth-watering cured ham, *jamón serrano*. This is naturally cured using traditional methods and the curing process takes a minimum of 14 months, after which the hams have acquired all their succulent aromas and flavours.

There are plenty of hotels and guest houses to choose from, although many establishments close down over some of the winter months. It's essential to check and reserve pre-arrival.

Trevélez is a place full of interest and contrasts: the lower part is quite touristy, as demonstrated by the number of coaches arriving during the spring to autumn period; the upper part is very traditional and it seems little has changed in the past decades.

Getting to Trevélez
Trevélez is reached by car from the main Granada to Motril motorway (A-44) in 1hr 15min (49km) using the A-348 and A-4132, passing through Lanjarón and turning left just on entering Órgiva. It is a beautiful and interesting journey.

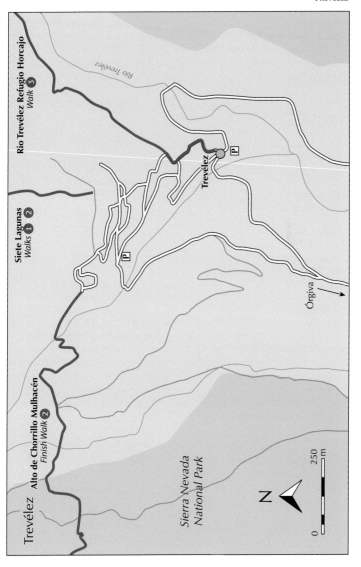

For Routes 1 and 2, if arriving by car, on entering Trevélez take the sign towards Barrio Alto and Barrio Medio. You'll find car parks on the edge of Barrio Alto. For Route 3 and the Río Trevélez it's best to park at the lower village.

There are three daily bus services from Granada: check the timetable at www.alsa.es/en/

ROUTE 1

Ascent of Alcazaba via Cañada de Siete Lagunas

Start/Finish	Car park at Barrio Medio, Trevélez (1540m)
Distance	22km
Total ascent	1770m
Grade	Tough
Time	11hr/2 days
Summits	Alcazaba
Water sources	Usually plentiful at Siete Lagunas and above, although a filter is advisable in high summer. Below Siete Lagunas there are many cattle herds, so it's better to carry more water rather than risk taking from lower sources.
Seasonal notes	In winter the caves at Siete Lagunas may well be filled with snow, requiring excavation. The waterfall at Chorreras Negras can be sheet ice in midwinter; in these conditions great care should be taken when ascending the flanking path. In July and August an early start is recommended from Trevélez to avoid the heat at lower altitudes.

Many visitors each year make the trip from one of the highest villages in Spain to the beautiful valley and lakes at Cañada de Siete Lagunas. Surrounded by the crags and cliffs of Mulhacén and Alcazaba, it is a spectacular place and in itself one of the classic walks of the Sierra Nevada. Many people camp here and then either return via the same route or continue to ascend Mulhacén or Alcazaba. As such this walk can either be done in one very long day or split into two shorter ones.

Alcazaba (3371m) is one of the finest mountains in the national park. Its very name, which translates as 'the fortress', invokes a sense of invincibility and impregnability. It is surrounded by cliffs, and yet to the south and east there are chinks in its armor that give pleasant ways to its lofty summit. There are three walking routes to the summit from Siete Lagunas, all of roughly the same length and time. The route via El Colaero is the most spectacular and is described here as the 'main' option; the other two alternatives are also given.

From the car park take the tarmac road 100m east to a market square, from where the route to the start of the track leaving town is well signposted. Walk up the street east past the Coviran store, turn left up the hill just before Hotel La Fragua, and then dogleg right. A large sign on the left indicates the start of the route as you leave the village.

After leaving the town proper the track rises slowly, passing through agricultural land before turning left up steepening slopes to join an irrigation channel (*acequia*) – the **Acequia Gorda**. Shortly after crossing the acequia, the path traverses up and across more open slopes towards the prow of **Prado Largo**.

After emerging from a young pine forest and crossing the **Acequia del Mingo**, the recently restored building at **La Campiñuela** (2410m) is reached (2hr, 5km). This is a useful landmark: make a mental note of the return path into the pine forest. (In descent it's easy to wander off on the wrong path, especially in mist.) In blizzards or bad weather the refuge makes a suitable emergency shelter.

The well-marked path continues into the valley of the curiously named Río Culo de Perro and crosses the river before ascending to the foot of the waterfall coming from the lip of Siete Lagunas, the **Chorreras Negras**. The path then zigzags its way up the steep northern side of the Chorreras, often muddy at the very top, before emerging over the lip and into the valley of **Siete Lagunas** (4hr 15min, 7.5km)

SIETE LAGUNAS

At this point, straight ahead lies the vast bulk of the east face of Mulhacén – the highest peak on mainland Spain – and to the right is Alcazaba. It is a magnificent sight. The lake directly ahead is Laguna Hondera, whose grassy banks make a delightful place to while away the hours.

For those intending to camp, there are plenty of possible sites. (Just a few metres south east of the lake are some natural caves that are often used.)

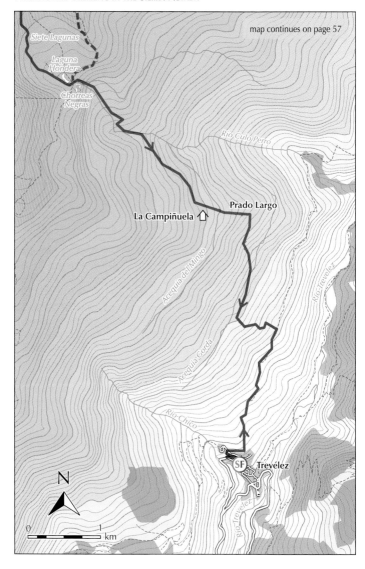

map continues on page 57

Siete Lagunas

Laguna
Hondera

Chorreas
Negras

Río Culo Perro

Prado Largo

La Campiñuela

Acequia del Mingo

Acequia Gorda

Río Chico

SF Trevélez

Río Trevélez

Río Trevélez

N

0   1 km

One of the delights of camping here is the morning sunrise over Laguna Hondera, with the line of the Sierra Nevada mountains stretching away to the east towards the distant hills of Almería.

Foxes can be a nuisance here in the summer (see 'General hazards' in the introduction); they are attracted to the food brought by overnight visitors. An alternative option would be to move up the gently sloping valley floor until you find a suitable bivouac site at one of the higher lakes.

It's a short but fine stroll up the valley to visit the other lakes. In the spring the valley is a mass of tumbling streams and rivers – a real delight. The upper lake is (not very originally) named Laguna Altera; it lies in a dramatic rocky hollow at the head of the valley beneath the peak of Puntal de Siete Lagunas (3244m).

From **Laguna Hondera** (lake), walk up the gently graded valley floor, passing alongside tumbling streams and tranquil lakes and aiming for the upper centre of the valley. There are some faint tracks but the way is obvious up to the upper basin, where the highest lake, **Laguna Altera**, lies encircled by cliffs and ridges.

Just before reaching the lake, take a track that heads north west up the steepening and rocky slopes, aiming for an obvious col between **Puntal de la Cornisa** (3307m) and Peñón del Globo (3279m). The gully leading up to this point is known as 'El Coleaero'; cairns mark the way, and although it is steep and loose the ascent is without difficulty. (At one point a hand may be required to assist upward progress, but this could hardly be called scrambling.)

El Colearo looks impossible from the lakes to the south east. Surely there can't be a walking route through those steep upper crags? The reality is that it is just a steep walk – but it is certainly a fascinating place, surrounded by rock walls and scenery reminiscent of the Skye Cuillin.

You may start to feel the altitude, but sooner than expected you arrive at the col, which is marked by a large cairn. Make a note of this place for the return journey – especially in misty conditions.

Ahead lies the fairly level plateau area leading to the summit, and the good path continues round the rim of the valley just below the ridge crest before the final climb up to the large summit cairn on **Alcazaba** at 3371m (6hr 15min, 11km).

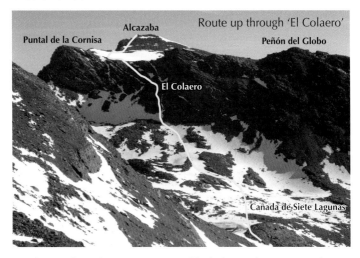

The **summit** is a fine viewpoint – possibly the best in the Sierra Nevada – with expansive views in all directions, although the plunging precipices of Mulhacén's north west face will no doubt draw the eye.

Alternative ascent via Peñón del Globo ridge

A track leaves Laguna Hondera at its south eastern side and goes north east towards the pinnacle of Piedra del Yunque east of Alcazaba. Follow this path for 10min until an easy ascent onto the broad south east ridge of Peñón del Globo can be made. There are signs of a path and the going is relatively easy until the ridge abuts steeper slopes running up to the summit (5hr 30min).

Now ascend on rocky and stony ground, avoiding some large boulders, until the ridge becomes more defined and eventually arrives at the summit of the **Peñón del Globo** at 3279m. From the summit continue along the ridge to the cairn at the col beyond, and the path coming up from the left from El Colaero. From here follow the main route description to the summit of **Alcazaba** (6hr 15min, 11km).

Alternative ascent via Meseta de las Borregas

This route should only be considered in fine, clear conditions as it passes through quite featureless terrain.

Take the alternative path described above to just below the steepening of the broad ridge of Peñón del Globo. Look for a small and obvious col to the

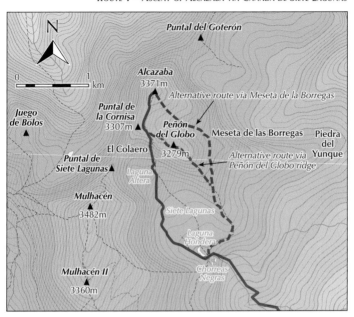

Looking south along the summit plateau to Puntal de la Cornisa, with the vast bulk of Mulhacén rising behind

Descending El Colaero gully

right (north) between the Loma de la Alcazaba and the ridge dropping down from Peñón del Globo: traverse across to this col on a good path. The col marks the entrance to the **Meseta de las Borregas** – the upper south east valley of Alcazaba (5hr).

After making a minor, almost imperceptible descent, cross the valley floor and ascend the slope opposite that joins the south east ridge, which is followed to the summit of **Alcazaba** (6hr 15min, 11km).

From the summit, the simplest descent – especially in mist – is to return the same way (via El Colaero) to **Siete Lagunas** (8hr). In clear weather you might choose to vary your route by reversing one of the alternatives described above. From Siete Lagunas, retrace your steps down the main route to return to **Trevélez**.

ROUTE 2

Ascent of Mulhacén via Cañada de Siete Lagunas

Start/Finish	Car park at Barrio Medio, Trevélez (1540m)
Distance	21km
Total ascent	1870m
Grade	Tough
Time	11hr/2 days
Summits	Mulhacén, Mulhacén II
Water sources	None after leaving Siete Lagunas
Seasonal notes	In winter this is a straightforward walk, although the steep slope immediately above Laguna Hondera can be icy. The waterfall at Chorreas Negras can be sheet ice and the flanking path frequently icy. Set off early in July and August to avoid the heat at lower altitudes.

From Trevélez the lure of the highest summit on mainland Spain, Mulhacén (3482m), is obvious. This walk can be done in one long tough day or as a more relaxing two-day jaunt, camping overnight beside the tranquil lakes at Siete Lagunas. (In summer the summit of Mulhacén can provide a wonderful place for a bivouac with superb sunsets and sunrises, although water would have to be carried up.)

A tough ascent up to Siete Lagunas is followed by the gentler eastern ridge walk up to the summit. From there a return is made down the south ridge to Alto del Chorrillo before turning east and descending steeply back to the village.

From the car park take the tarmac road 100m east to a market square, from where the route to the start of the track leaving town is well signposted. Walk up the street east past the Coviran store, turn left up the hill just before Hotel La Fragua, and then dogleg right. A large sign on the left indicates the start of the route as you leave the village.

After leaving the town proper the track rises slowly, passing through agricultural land before turning left up steepening slopes to join an irrigation channel (*acequia*) – the **Acequia Gorda**. Shortly after crossing the acequia, the path traverses up and across more open slopes towards the prow of **Prado Largo**.

Iced-up waterfalls of Chorreras Negras in late autumn

After emerging from a young pine forest and crossing the **Acequia del Mingo**, the recently restored building at **La Campiñuela** (2410m) is reached (2hr, 5km). In blizzards or bad weather the refuge makes a suitable emergency shelter.

The well-marked path continues into the valley of the curiously named Río Culo de Perro and crosses the river before ascending to the foot of the waterfall coming from the lip of Siete Lagunas, the **Chorreras Negras**. The path then zig-zags its way up the steep northern side of the Chorreras, often muddy at the very top, before emerging over the lip and into the valley of **Siete Lagunas** (4hr 15min, 7.5km).

SIETE LAGUNAS

At this point, straight ahead lies the vast bulk of the east face of Mulhacén – the highest peak on mainland Spain – and to the right is Alcazaba. It is a magnificent sight. The lake directly ahead is Laguna Hondera, whose grassy banks make a delightful place to while away the hours.

For those intending to camp, there are plenty of possible sites. (Just a few metres south east of

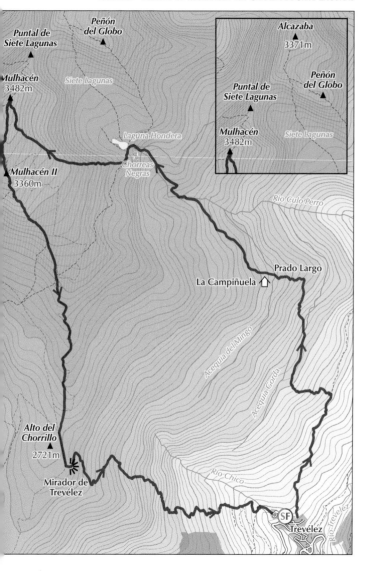

the lake are some natural caves that are often used.) One of the delights of camping here is the morning sunrise over Laguna Hondera, with the line of the Sierra Nevada mountains stretching away to the east towards the distant hills of Almería.

Foxes can be a nuisance here in the summer (see 'General hazards' in the introduction); they are attracted to the food brought by overnight visitors. An alternative option would be to move up the gently sloping valley floor until you find a suitable bivouac site at one of the higher lakes.

It's a short but fine stroll up the valley to visit the other lakes. In the spring the valley is a mass of tumbling streams and rivers – a real delight. The upper lake is (not very originally) named Laguna Altera; it lies in a dramatic rocky hollow at the head of the valley beneath the peak of Puntal de Siete Lagunas (3244m).

From **Laguna Hondera** at Siete Lagunas, take the well-marked path that zigzags up the steep hillside south of the lake to reach a small col, where a large cairn marks the spot at which the eastern traverse path joins. Looking ahead, the ridge rises and then curves to the right towards the summit.

> From just above here it is possible to see why the **Río Culo Perro** might have been so-named: its literal translation is 'dog's arse river', and when you see the shape of Laguna Hondera from some angles on this ridge it does indeed take the shape of a dog – from the rear of which comes the river cascading down over the waterfalls of Chorreras Negras.

Continue up the slope above the col, which seems relentless as the altitude begins to make itself known. Small cairns mark the track, which is faint in places. There is at times a choice of path; in mist or snow keep the escarpment on your right-hand side until the broader slopes of the upper mountain are reached and the track coming up from the Mirador de Trevélez to the south is joined. Turn right and follow easy slopes to the summit of **Mulhacén** at 3482m (6hr 15min, 10km).

> The **east face** of Mulhacén presents the shortest route from Siete Lagunas to the summit – but the terrain is rough and loose, there's no real path, and the ascent is very arduous. Nobody but a masochist would really want to do it in summer, but in winter with hard snow it makes for a delightful ascent. Under these conditions too, a descent from the summit back to the lakes can be made very rapidly.

On the upper east ridge, nearing the summit

Descend gently south on a well-marked and well-cairned path to the south summit (**Mulhacén II**, 6hr 45min, 11km), then more steeply to join the old road at a junction with a dirt track leading to Refugio Poqueira. This is where the national park bus from Capileira drops walkers during the summer months. Follow the road for 200m, passing east of **Alto de Chorrillo** (2721m). At a sign, leave the road and follow the path east to the rocks overlooking Trevélez. This is the **Mirador de Trevélez** (8hr, 15.5km)

The appropriately named **Mirador de Trevélez** provides a convenient

MULHACÉN

On a fine day the views from the summit are tremendous in all directions. The Sierras of Mágina, Cazorla and Segura are prominent to the north, with the main ridge of the Sierra Nevada stretching north east past Alcazaba and turning east before dropping down towards the desert badlands and plains of Almería. The Mediterranean Sea sparkles to the south, accompanied by a possible sighting of the Rif mountains and coastline of Morocco. To the west the main ridge line leads onto the bulk of Veleta, and Granada can be seen nestling far below. It's also worth peering (with great care) over the huge precipice of the north west face, which plummets 600m to the lake at Laguna de la Mosca.

On a weekend in the summer months it can be very busy here, but the lover of solitude will be rewarded on a winter or midweek visit outside of the holiday periods.

Ruined buildings can be seen close to the summit; they were originally built in 1879 and used to establish the first geodesic link – the shortest possible line on a curved surface (ie the earth) – between Europe and Africa, connecting the peninsula with Morocco. This is also the reason for the old access road to the peak. Some of these buildings later served as a refuge for the first mountaineers.

place to shelter if high winds are blowing from the west across the exposed slopes above.

Continue on the path as it drops down the steep hillside in a series of zig-zags. As you near the village, cross some roads and join the GR7; the route is clearly marked and eventually emerges at the highest point of the north west corner of **Trevélez** (Barrio Alto).

ROUTE 3
Round of the Río Juntillas and Trevélez valleys

Start/Finish	Car park in lower village, Trevélez
Distance	38km; easier alternative: 35km
Total ascent	2180m; easier alternative: 1670m
Grade	Tough; easier alternative: challenging
Time	17hr/2–3 days; easier alternative: 12hr 30min/2 days
Summits	Puntal de Vacares, Pico del Cuervo, Pico de la Justica o Atalaya, Puntal de los Cuartos, Tajos Negros de Cobatillas, Puntal de Juntillas, Piedra de los Ladrones
Water sources	Water usually available at Río Juntillas, Laguna de Juntillas and Río Puerto de Jérez
Seasonal notes	There can be severe icing east of Puntal de Juntillas, with vertical cliffs lying in wait just to the north in Barranco del Alhorí.

A multi-day trekking route for lovers of solitude and wild scenery, covering some unfrequented sections of the Sierra Nevada. The circular route goes up the Río Juntillas to the main ridge and descends the Río Puerto de Jérez. It features 3000m peaks and remote situations, with few other people likely to be seen above Refugio Horcajo.

Camping is possible at Refugio Horcajo, Laguna de Vacares and Lagunas de Juntillas. Various delectable camping and bivouac sites can also be found alongside the Río Juntillas and Río Puerto de Jérez.

An alternative ascent to the main ridge line via Río Juntillas is described for those wanting an easier route or as a backup in poor weather conditions.

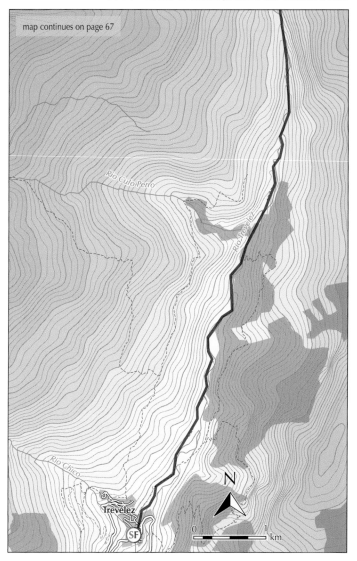

map continues on page 67

Río Culo Perro

Río Trevélez

Río Chico

Trevélez

SF

N

0   1 km.

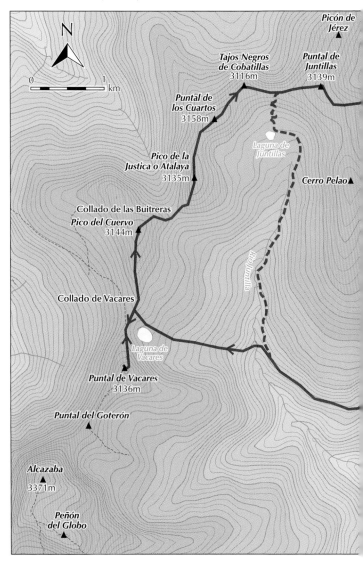

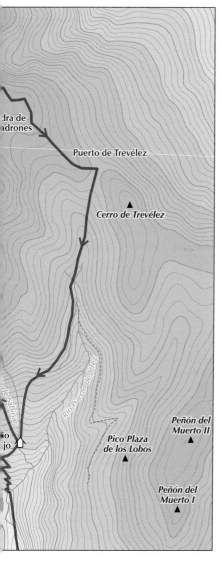

dra de
adrones

Puerto de Trevélez

Cerro de Trevélez ▲

Pico Plaza
de los Lobos
▲

Peñón del
Muerto II
▲

Peñón del
Muerto I
▲

Río Puerto de Jérez

de Sabinar

io
jo

From the car park in the lower village, go up through the right-hand side of Trevélez to reach and take a well-defined road that heads north, keeping on the west side of the Río Trevélez. After 1.2km and before the road crosses the Río Trevélez, take a path on the left. This develops into a meandering track that continues along the west side of the river.

Caballeros (horsemen), accompanied by their friendly dogs, frequently use this valley trail to access their animals grazing in the lush, high pastures near the junction of the Río Juntillas and Río Puerto de Jérez.

After 5km the **Río Culo Perro** joins from the left and the path starts to slowly ascend the narrowing valley, crossing over the Río Trevélez via a series of bridges. A small descent leads to a grassy area, old ruins and bridge at the junction of the Río Juntillas and Río Puerto de Jérez rivers. Take the stony and signposted path rising north from the bridge, and **Refugio Horcajo** (2220m) is reached (3hr, 9.5km).

A moody evening at Refugio Horcajo

The **refuge** is in reasonable condition and is set in a superb location. For those starting the trek at midday, this would be a convenient place to spend the night, with water available from Barranco del Sabinar alongside.

From the refuge trend north west to reach an irrigation channel, which is followed to a junction with the **Río Juntillas** at 2500m. There is another possible bivouac place here among the boulders above the river. From here the route will climb up to and traverse the mountains ahead from left to right.

Cross the Río Juntillas at the junction with the irrigation channel – this may be difficult if in spate – and take the initially steep path that runs north of the Reguera de los Caños stream and emerges at a lake, **Laguna de Vacares** (2900m), and hence to the col, **Collado de Vacares** (2970m; 6hr, 14km).

Puntal de Vacares now lies to the south, but note that the ascent is harder and longer than it looks from the col. The way ahead has paths on both sides of the ridge; that to the right is easier than the left, which requires some initial simple scrambling over a few steps on loose ground. After that the ridge broadens and leads steeply to the summit of **Puntal de Vacares** (3136m; 7hr 15min, 15km). The summit is a fine viewpoint – especially towards the impregnable looking wall of the north face of Alcazaba. Return the same way to Collado de Vacares.

Heading north from the col, ascend some rocky sections of ridge to reach **Pico del Cuervo** (3144m). From here a short but steep descent – initially north and then east – leads to **Collado de las Buitreras**, and then another steep ascent just right of the main ridge line leads to **Pico de la Justica** (3135m). Faster progress will now be made as the route continues over the peaks of **Puntal de los Cuartos** (3156m) and **Tajos Negros de Cobatillas** (3116m) to join the easier alternative route ascending from Laguna de Juntillas to the south. The ridge rises easily eastwards to arrive at **Puntal de Juntillas** (3139m; 11hr 30min, 21km).

> The **view** is expansive northwards to the valleys of Lavaderos de la Reina (north west) and Barranco del Alhóri (north east). To the south west, Alcazaba, Mulhacén and Veleta dominate the skyline.

Easier alternative to Puntal de Juntillas following the Río Juntillas
This is a much easier option and safer in poor weather or mist.

From the junction of the Río Juntillas with the irrigation channel, pick up the path that rises on the eastern side of the river and follow it until it emerges on flatter ground near **Laguna de Juntillas** (2920m). Take the steep zig-zag path north of the lake and climb 200m to the main ridge line of the Sierra Nevada, to a point just a few hundred metres west of **Puntal de Juntillas** (3139m; 7hr, 17km). It is a simple matter to gain the summit and rejoin the main route from here.

Purists may want to pick up the peak of Picón de Jérez (3090m) just 1km to the north-north east, or Cerro Pelao (3181m) 1.5km to the south. To continue on the main route, though, head east from Puntal de Juntillas.

The character of the route softens as the ridge becomes broad and the mountains less jagged. To the east the mountain ridge undulates away into the distance before dropping down to the desert badlands of Almería. Descend over the tundra-like terrain – bearing in mind that there are steep slopes to the north (Barranco del Alhorí) that could catch out the unwary in winter – and pass over the minor peak of **Piedra de los Ladrones** (2944m) before turning south east and descending easily to the pass of **Puerto de Trevélez** 2800m. Turn right (south) here and descend alongside the **Río Puerto de Jérez**.

After passing some delectable camping sites, at 2500m the path starts to leave the river and trend round to the south west above Acequia de Sabinar. Just before arriving at the gorge of Barranco de Sabinar, drop down and cross the *acequia* (irrigation channel). The path now leads easily down to the **Refugio Horcajo** (14hr 30min, 28km).

Follow the long valley of the **Río Trevélez** for about 2hr, retracing your steps to the village of **Trevélez**.

CAPILEIRA

Traversing the hillside with the valley of the Río Seco and Raspones beyond (Route 4)

Capileira, at 1450m, is the highest of the three white villages perched on shelves high in the gorge of Barranco de Poqueira. It forms a convenient base for walking routes in the south of the range, and especially for the popular ascents of Mulhacén via Refugio Poqueira.

There are superb views from Capileira down the *barranco* (gorge) and across to the mountains of the Sierra de Lujar. The Sierra Nevada rises behind the village, with the peak of Veleta (3394m) prominent and towering above.

There are plenty of accommodation options, as well as bars, restaurants and souvenir shops. In particular the Meson Poqueira and Finca Los Llanos provide good value accommodation for walkers. The village's steep, narrow and twisting streets contain many springs, providing refreshing mountain waters. It can get quite busy with tourists in the summer months, at weekends and during *fiestas* (public holidays).

The Sierra Nevada National Park information office is on the left when entering the town, just after the initial car parks and before the Meson Poqueira hotel, bar and restaurant. This is the point from which the national park bus service operates in the summer months. See 'Getting around' in this book's introduction.

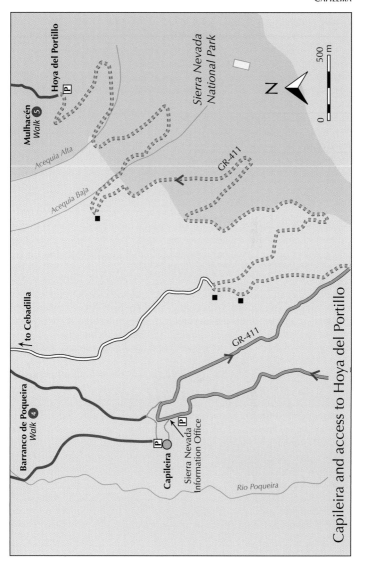

Capileira and access to Hoya del Portillo

Getting to Capileira

Capileira is reached by car from the main Granada to Motril motorway (A-44) using the A-348 and A-4132, passing through Lanjarón and turning left just on entering Órgiva. After 20min the road enters a massive gorge (Barranco de Poqueira) with the three white villages – Pampaneira, Bubión and Capileira – high above at the end of the valley. Follow the main road, passing through Pampaneira, and 5min later (just before a petrol station) turn left to Bubión and Capileira. The village is 1hr and 35km from the motorway.

There are three daily bus services from Granada; check the timetable at www.alsa.es/en/

Route 4 starts from the village itself, while Route 5 starts 700m above it at the trailhead of Hoya del Portillo.

Getting to Hoya del Portillo

From the national park information office in Capileira (next to Meson Poqueira), follow the GR-411 out of the village and steadily uphill. After 2km the tarmac finishes and a rough dirt road begins. After another 1km, just above some horse riding stables, a road branches left to La Cebadilla and Central Electricá del Poqueira. Fork right.

The road now climbs up the mountainside in a series of long zig-zags, alternating between forest and open hillside. There are some stunning views towards the Pico del Tajo de los Machos to Veleta ridge from here. After a further 7.5km you arrive at a barrier across the road and a large car park: this is the forestry station at Hoya del Portillo (2150m), 30min and 10.5km from Capileira.

ROUTE 4

Barranco de Poqueira circular

Start/Finish	National park information office, Capileira
Distance	20km
Total ascent	930m
Grade	Challenging
Time	8hr
Water sources	Río Poqueira, Río Mulhacén and Río Veleta
Seasonal notes	Under hard ice or fresh soft snow the route alongside the acequias (irrigation channels) can be tough going.

A 'must-do' circular offering a contrasting day walk from Capileira, this route provides a good introduction to the delights of the Sierra Nevada. It initially follows irrigation channels on the eastern side of the gorge, before returning high above on its western side and joining the river towards the end.

There is a short (20m) section of narrow path with some degree of exposure, but this is protected by a fixed cable and fence.

Exit the town from its north west side by following either Calle Mulhacén or Calle Castillo. Take the path that leaves the northern side of the village; this is the main path to La Cebadilla and Refugio Poqueira that passes high above the eastern side of the Río Poqueira.

After 1km there is a **circular construction** (an *alberca*, used for water storage); just before this, leave the path by following a dirt road up to the right. This meets the main Capileira/Cebadilla dirt road. Turn right and then immediately left up a path inside a forest break which leads to a further dirt road.

Follow the dirt road for 1km until another path comes in from the right; take this, which leads out of the forest and onto the open hillside. The path climbs gently beneath some broken crags to cross an irrigation channel (**Acequia Baja**) and rises up to join the higher **Acequia Alta**. A short distance on are the buildings at **Corrales de Pitres** (2hr, 5km).

The path continues a little below and west of Acequia Alta to pass just above **Cortijo de Las Tomas** and, contouring the hillside, to reach the **dam** over the Río Mulhacén (3hr 30min, 8.5km).

Short cut to the Central Eléctrica de Poqueira

At Cortijo de Las Tomas it is possible to drop down and reach the Central Eléctrica de Poqueira via Río Naute on a good, well-marked track. This route avoids the short exposed path across the cliff face and saves 2km in distance, 200m of ascent and an hour in time.

To continue on the main route, cross the dam; the way ahead is now obvious on a horizontal path cutting through the near-vertical cliff. Just as the exposure begins to build, a secure cable is provided to assist with progress. The going is really quite simple – even for those of a nervous disposition – although there is one place where you have to resort to a hands-and-knees crawl in order to pass under an overhanging rock protuberance. A few minutes of excitement and you're back on the path again, difficulties passed. In 2015 the national park erected a

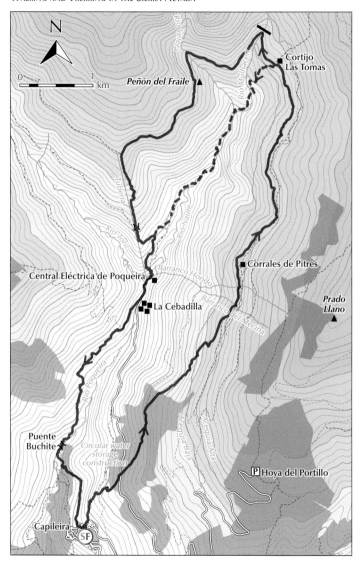

Looking south from the easy trail to the top of Hydro 'Tubería'

fence alongside the cable, reducing the exposure and consequent trembling of the knees!

The path now contours into the valley of the **Río Veleta** and gradually descends to cross it by another dam and irrigation channel. Don't follow the acequia here; instead you will find a good path above Peñón del Fraile that rises steadily up to a small col between the obvious large prow of rock ahead and the main mountainside. Once over the col, a short descent is followed by a superb path that leads without difficulties to the upper building of Hydro 'Tubería' (5hr, 12km).

Descend alongside and to the east of the Tubería until you reach the **bridge** at Puente Toril. Keep left and drop down until you reach the main path to Refugio Poqueira; here turn right and descend to the **Central Eléctrica de Poqueira** hydro station (6hr, 14.5km).

Just south of the **Central Eléctrica de Poqueira hydroelectric plant** is the abandoned hamlet of La Cebadilla, which was built to house the workers and their families. The plant was completed in 1957; after that, most people migrated to the cities (except for a few old men who remained in their houses, choosing to enjoy the solitude of the Poqueira valley). Now there is no one left and the plant is no longer the modern and imposing construction that it was in its day.

The return to the village takes a well-marked trail west of the river. Some 200m after leaving the station take the road to the right which rises to a bend, from which a path leaves the road to the left. Follow this pleasant track down to the bridge at **Puente Buchite** before rising steeply back up to **Capileira**.

ROUTE 5
Ascent of Mulhacén from Hoya del Portillo

Start/Finish	Forestry station, Hoya del Portillo
Distance	23.5km
Total ascent	1330m
Grade	Tough
Time	8hr 30min
Summits	Mulhacén II, Mulhacén
Water sources	Spring above Puerto Molina, Laguna de la Caldera (off-route)
Seasonal notes	Makes for a very long route in winter depending on where the snow line begins – if it's low, stay overnight at Refugio Poqueira. Beware possible avalanche dangers at Paso de los Franceses. The western flank of Mulhacén can be hard ice and accidents have occurred there. If in doubt, return using the broad south ridge.

From the Alpujarras in the south, the ascent of Mulhacén – at 3482m the highest peak on mainland Spain – can be done in one long day in the summer. This route avoids using the national park bus and traverses the mountain without ever covering the same ground twice.

There is a well-signposted track going up left of the forestry station; take this and head north uphill through the forest on a good track. Leave the top end of the forest, and just before meeting a forest break (with a signpost beyond signalling the way to Refugio Poqueira) zig-zag back right and upwards to reach an old road. Follow this dirt track past the wonderful viewpoint of **Puerto Molina** (45min, 2km).

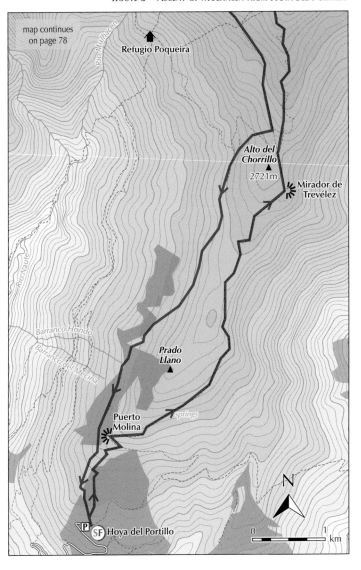

map continues
on page 78

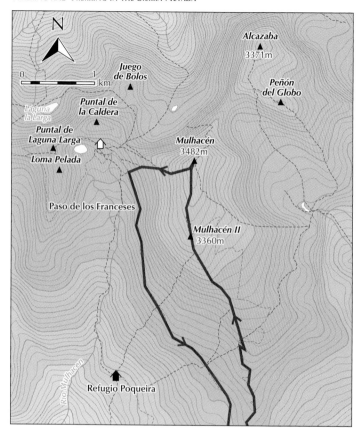

Puerto Molina is worth a short stop. Not only for the fabulous **views** towards the Sierra Nevada but also for the information boards which detail the geological history of the area as well as its most outstanding fauna.

Follow the road. After 30min reliable springs are passed on the left. Two hours (6.5km) after starting you will arrive close to **Alto de Chorrillo**, with **Mirador de Trevélez** just 50m to the east by some rocks overlooking the town. This is a good place to take a break and enjoy the view – and to get out of the prevailing south west winds.

Having taken in the view, follow the road north. At a junction, take the path veering off to the right (the left-hand path goes to Refugio Poqueira, 30min). This is the main route to the summit from the south and it is well marked due to the thousands that ascend this way each year – the national park has placed cairns every 25m or so.

About 20min after leaving the road and starting the ascent, a 3m-high post some 50m off to the west of the path marks the site of an old **Civil War bunker** supremely camouflaged into the surrounding rocks. It has a commanding view over the whole of the southern slopes of the Sierra Nevada and is worth a look. It could also be used as an emergency shelter. (There's a spade provided to dig the entrance out of the winter snows.)

It's a steady but relentless ascent to Mulhacén's south summit – **Mulhacén II** (3360m). To the east of the path are traces of an old road ascending from a plateau at 3000m.

The next objective, **Mulhacén**'s main summit (3482m; 4hr 30min, 12km), is an easy 1km away to the north. When you get there, if you're not prone to vertigo, glance over the summit rocks and down the north face to Laguna de la Mosca, nestling 600m below.

The cliffs of the north face drop precipitously from the summit of Mulhacén

From the summit, drop 50m south to a point where two adjacent cairns mark the start of the west flank descent. Follow the path west; it steepens until the full extent of the west flank is seen below. There are great views across to the mountain ridges from Puntal de la Caldera to Veleta. This is an unrelenting descent of 500m in a series of steep zig-zags, but it's quick and you should be down at the old road (5hr 30min, 13km) in 45min.

Turn left (south) on the old road, which passes over **Paso de los Franceses** and eventually nears Alto de Chorrillo and the ascent route. Some 400m before **Alto de Chorrillo**, bear right and down over pathless terrain to meet the road that goes from the Poqueira hut to Alto de Chorrillo. At the first left hand bend in the track, take a path traversing south. Follow this along the mountainside; it passes through a forested area before arriving at a forest break above Hoya del Portillo. After fresh snowfall the forests around Hoya del Portillo make an excellent location for snowshoeing.

Follow the firebreak down. It's a bit rough, but no rougher than the Mulhacén slopes tackled previously. After 10min you'll see a small cairn on the left (looking down) that signifies a small path entering the forest. Take this path, which is very faint or non-existent in places, and after a gently descending traverse you will reach the forest road and visitor car park at **Hoya del Portillo**.

Start of the south ridge at Alto de Chorrillo

REFUGIO POQUEIRA

The ring of peaks surrounding Laguna de la Caldera (Route 7)

The walk to Refugio Poqueira from Capileira (5hr, 10km, 1120m ascent)

The refuge is the start-point for all of the walks in this section. The following is a recommended route to the refuge – especially if there are high winds or bad weather, as it is relatively sheltered in the valley of the Poqueira river. Note, however, that the final part above Cortijo de las Tomas is fully exposed to the elements and is unavoidable.

On foot, exit Capileria from its north west side, either by following Calle Mulhacén or Calle Castillo. A path leaves the north side of the village and rises gently to join a dirt road coming in from the right, which is followed to the ruins of **La Cebadilla** (1hr).

From here, follow the path as it crosses the river, turns right and very shortly emerges at the **Central Eléctrica del Poqueira** plant. Pass by the plant, and at the end of the concrete road follow a large sign which points the way ahead up a steep zig-zag track, very quickly gaining height above the Río Poqueira.

The undulating track eventually drops down to recross the river via a couple of bridges before climbing again steadily to meet another bridge at the junction with the **Río Veleta**, which comes in from the left (north west). Cross this bridge

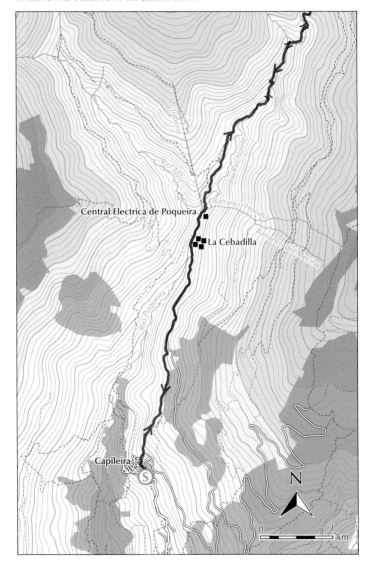

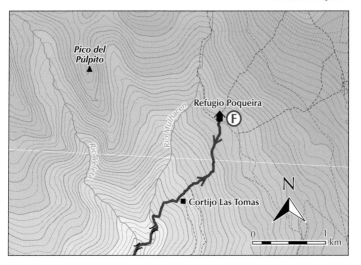

and ascend to a further bridge that crosses the lower reaches of the **Río Mulhacén**. This is a superb place to take a breather and admire the scenery before tackling the next stage.

Now the hard work begins as the path steepens and rises left of the stream (Barranco Peñón Negro) directly behind **Cortijo de Las Tomas** (4hr). During the ascent, two irrigation channels are crossed (Acequia Baja and Acequia Alta); after Acequia Alta and a rising traverse to the left, **Refugio Poqueira** comes into view and is reached after 10min on a path marked by coloured poles which provide assistance in thick mist or on snow-covered ground.

By car

Those intending to park at La Cebadilla should keep on the main road through Capileira, and after 3km (and above the horse riding stables) turn left signposted 'Cebadilla'. The road deteriorates but is normally suitable for cars if care is taken. The walk from La Cebadilla to the refuge takes about 4hr.

83

ROUTE 6
Ascent of Mulhacén from Refugio Poqueira

Start/Finish	Refugio Poqueira
Distance	9.5km
Total ascent	990m
Grade	Challenging
Time	5hr 30min
Summits	Mulhacén, Mulhacén II
Water sources	Río Mulhacén
Seasonal notes	The west flank of Mulhacén can be hard ice and accidents have occurred here. Enquire at the refuge for the latest conditions and if in doubt use the south ridge for both ascent and descent.

This is the classic traverse of the highest mountain on mainland Spain: starting from Refugio Poqueira and ascending the steep west flank, then descending via the long south ridge.

From the refuge, follow the trail north west as it gradually descends to join the **Río Mulhacén**. Paths ascend both sides of the river, but the path to its west is perhaps preferable; follow this to a junction with the old road, passing through some delightful *borreguiles* (high-mountain meadows) in its upper reaches.

The **old road** that crosses the Sierra Nevada used to be the highest road in Europe, but since the Sierra Nevada gained national park status it has been closed at both ends. Every year it becomes more and more rock-covered and is slowly but surely turning back into a more natural state. It does help to provide quick access from the north and south, however it can be overrun by mountain bikers as soon as the snow clears in July and throughout August. In winter the road can be covered completely by high-angled snow for many months.

The west flank of Mulhacén towers above you and there are two options at the junction, each representing a similar time and distance: you can either take the well-cairned route directly to Mulhacén's summit (see below), or, much

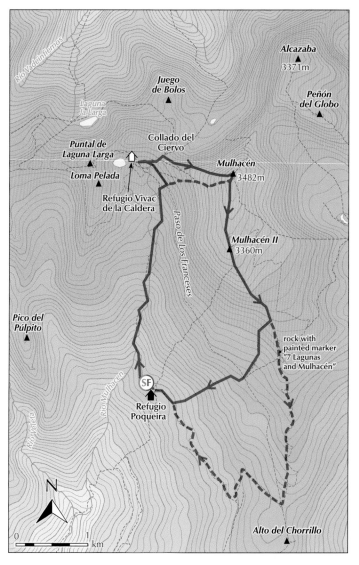

better, you can visit the dramatically situated Refugio Vivac de la Caldera and Collado del Ciervo before taking a straightforward but breathtaking ridge route to the summit.

Follow the old road for 400m and then take the path on the right, leading in a further 200m to the **refuge** – so-named as the lake of the same name sits in a bowl below, surrounded by high mountain ridges. A path leads north east from the refuge to the col, **Collado del Ciervo** (2hr, 4km), which provides a superb vista of Mulhacén's north face with Laguna de la Mosca sitting at its base. Alcazaba looks wonderful from here too. Most visitors to Mulhacén, possibly struggling up the west flank path, will be unaware of this view.

From the col, a track can be taken to join the main west flank path at half-height – but the best route to the summit hugs the junction of the north and west faces and keeps to the ridge edge. This route can look a bit intimidating from below, but it is in fact simple hands-in-pockets walking, with no scrambling involved – and to the left is that amazing drop down the north face.

The ridge lands you very close to the actual summit of **Mulhacén** (3482m; 3hr 30min, 5km), just a short stroll away. In summer, before joining the noisy throng surrounding the summit cairn, take a long look back down your ascent route – or better still, stay where you are and eat your lunch in peace!

A visit to Collado del Ciervo opens up dramatic alpine views to the north

At the top of the west flank, with Veleta in the distance and cloud inversion below (Photo: Andrew Phillips)

Direct route to the summit

From the old road, simply follow the interminable zig-zag path as it climbs the 450 vertical metres to the summit of **Mulhacén** (3hr 30min, 5km). The path seems never-ending but in fact 1hr 30min or less will see you on the top.

To return to Refugio Poqueira, follow an easy path south towards Mulhacén II. Just before the south summit, ignore the semblance of a road that turns off eastwards and pass just left of the summit cairn. Take the path that descends just west of the ridge line into a shallow bowl, which you traverse.

Follow the path as it switches to the east of the ridge line and descends to the 3000m level, where you meet an old road coming in from the east. At a corner of the road and junction of the Mulhacén path you will see 'Mulhacén' and '7 Lagunas' markers painted on a rock; at this point take a faint path south west and down some scree to cross the old trans-Sierra Nevada road before dropping down a shallow gully to a dirt road. Turn right to reach the **refuge**.

Alternative descent

A longer (by 1hr, 3km) but safer descent from the painted stone marker in mist or poor conditions is to continue down the main, well-cairned path to **Alto de Chorrillo**. From here a signposted dirt road leads to the refuge without difficulty.

ROUTE 7
The Caldera peaks

Start/Finish	Refugio Poqueira
Distance	10km
Total ascent	680m
Grade	Challenging
Time	6hr
Summits	Puntal de la Caldera, Puntal de Laguna Larga, Loma Pelada
Water sources	Río Mulhacén, Laguna de la Caldera
Seasonal notes	The east ridge of Puntal de la Caldera makes for a straightforward winter ascent.

This route visits two worthwhile objectives, often neglected or bypassed in the rush to climb Mulhacén. Both Puntal de la Caldera and Puntal de Laguna Larga give impressive vistas over the northern precipices of the Sierra Nevada. There is some simple scrambling (mostly avoidable) up the east ridge of Puntal de la Caldera.

From the refuge, follow the trail north west as it gradually descends to join the **Río Mulhacén**. Paths on both sides of the river lead upwards to join the old road, which is then followed towards Refugio Vivac de la Caldera. The refuge is set in a spectacular location surrounded by high mountain ridges.

Some 50m before the refuge, cairned paths lead east, rising to the pass of **Collado del Ciervo** (2hr, 4km). A spectacular view of the precipitous northern faces of Mulhacén and Alcazaba opens up here with the diminutive Laguna de la Mosca nestling below.

From the pass, the ridge ahead to the summit of Puntal de la Caldera is very broken; there are sections of scree interspersed with rocky outcrops. A faint path may be encountered at times, but a choice has to be made to either take the ridge direct (simple scrambling) or avoid the ridge crest to the south (rough walking). The ridge crest provides the best views, and any awkward or exposed sections can readily be avoided to the south.

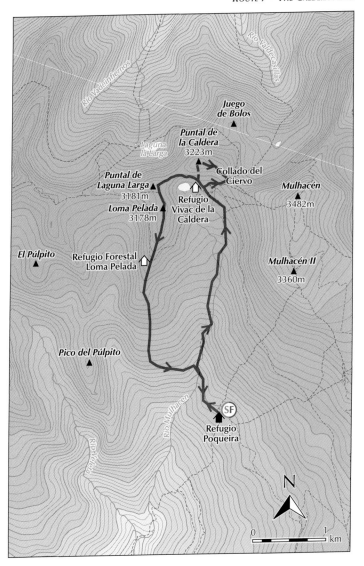

Near the summit of Puntal de la Caldera, looking west across to Veleta

Just before the summit a level section along the crest provides the most exposure – or it is possible to downclimb a short step to the left (south). The summit of **Puntal de la Caldera** (3323m; 3hr, 4.5km) is just beyond.

The ridge can be followed directly to Puntal de Laguna Larga but it involves much higher-grade scrambling. This walk returns to Refugio Vivac de la Caldera by either of two options: back down the east ridge to Collado del Ciervo, or via scree slopes south from the summit directly in line with the refuge.

From behind the **refuge** (3hr 45min, 5.5km), a good path wends its way improbably between the crags and traverses up to the col between Puntal de Laguna Larga (3178m) and Loma Pelada. At the col, turn right and reach the summit of **Puntal de Laguna Larga** a few minutes' easy walk away to the north.

The vast difference in angle between the seemingly vertical northern slopes and the much more gentle southern ones is seen at its best from the summit of **Puntal de Laguna Larga**. Way below, tiny lakes nestle in glacial hollows. Although slightly lower than its neighbour to the south, the northern summit is much the preferred viewpoint with expansive and dramatic vistas in all directions.

From here it's a mere 300m easy stroll south to the summit of **Loma Pelada** (3181m; 4hr 30min, 6.5km), from where you walk south over generally pathless terrain, following the well-defined ridge, until you reach **Refugio Forestal Loma Pelada** just south of the old trans-Sierra Nevada road.

Some maps and most locals call this building, more appropriately, **'Refugio Villavientos'** – and it does make a convenient place to spend the night in winter. In summer there are no water sources close enough to warrant staying here.

Continue south down the long, broad ridge from the refuge on mostly pathless terrain, until at around 2700m you meet a track coming in from the Río Seco to the right. Turn left to the **Río Mulhacén** and hence back to **Refugio Poqueira**.

ROUTE 8
Around Mulhacén via the Vasar and Siete Lagunas

Start/Finish	Refugio Poqueira
Distance	12km
Total ascent	900m
Grade	Challenging
Time	6hr
Summits	Puntal de Siete Lagunas
Water sources	Río Mulhacén, Laguna de la Caldera, Fuente del Viejo Lobo, Siete Lagunas
Seasonal notes	The Vasar is usually clear of snow by mid July until the first snows arrive in October or November. Avoid the Vasar if snow lies anywhere on the north face. The eastern traverse of Mulhacén can have large snowfields well into June.
Note	A helmet is advised for the Vasar, due to the possibility of rock being dislodged from the summit area above.

This circular walk takes an improbable-looking horizontal shelf (Vasar de Mulhacén) across Mulhacén's seemingly vertical north face to reach the peak of Puntal de Siete Lagunas. It is an adrenaline-filled but very straightforward walk to a superb summit with only one short section where the hands might need to leave the pockets. A head for heights is advisable, though.

The route continues round into Siete Lagunas and returns to the refuge via the eastern traverse of Mulhacén. All in all, this is a relatively unknown route that visits some remarkable situations on rarely visited paths.

From the refuge, follow the trail north west as it gradually descends to join the **Río Mulhacén**. Paths on both sides of the river lead upwards to join the old road, which is then followed towards Refugio Vivac de la Caldera. Some 50m before the refuge, turn east on cairned paths to the col, **Collado del Ciervo** (2hr, 4km). A spectacular view of the precipitous northern faces of Mulhacén and Alcazaba opens up, with the diminutive Laguna de la Mosca nestling below.

From the col, follow a path just right of the west ridge of Mulhacén, passing two small cols to arrive at yet another col below a large cliff, marked by a large cairn. The way along the **Vasar** is obvious from here – and may look somewhat daunting to the uninitiated!

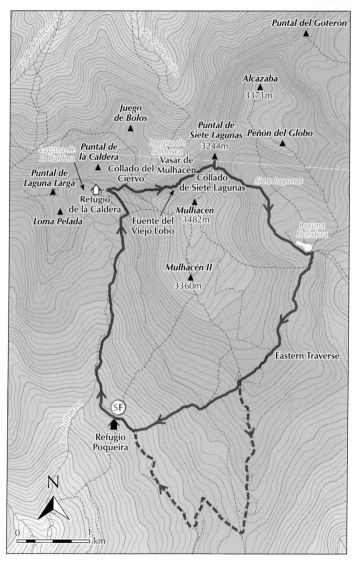

Embarking along the initial section of the Vasar (Photo: Andrew Phillips)

The Vasar makes use of a narrow horizontal shelf crossing the face at about 3150m, sandwiched between vertical walls above and below.

The path winds its way in and out of the twists and turns on the north face. Once started, and the realisation dawns that all is well and it is indeed quite easy, you will begin to enjoy the incredibly dramatic situation. Surprisingly there is little exposure – although you are always aware of the steep cliffs above and below you – and the surprises keep on coming, as right in the centre of the face you meet a spring (**Fuente del Viejo Lobo**) which produces refreshingly cold water even in the height of summer.

Due to its unique location, this path is a botanist's delight. There are many **endemic plants** to be found, including the Sierra Nevada violet (*Viola crassiuscula*). Various types of lichens and mosses exist in the unique conditions found on the face. The Sierra Nevada poppy (*Papaver lapeyrousianum*) has also been spotted along this track.

There's just one short step that requires a steady head for heights: round a protruding boulder that crosses the path. Those of a nervous disposition could clamber round the back of the boulder instead without difficulty.

The gently rising path reaches the end of the Vasar and meets a zig-zag path coming up the scree from Laguna de la Mosca to the left (El Corredor de Siete Lagunas). Simple walking leads to a col, **Collado de Siete Lagunas**, between Mulhacén and Puntal de Siete Lagunas. The summit of **Puntal de Siete Lagunas** (3244m; 3hr 30min, 5.5km) is a 5min walk away and is one of the finest spots in the Sierra Nevada, surrounded by crags and cliffs.

Return to the col and drop east into **Siete Lagunas** on a well-marked path zig-zagging through the upper screes until the first of the lakes is met, then take a gentle stroll down through the remaining lakes to **Laguna Hondera** (4hr 30min, 7.5km) at the entrance to the valley. This section is magnificent – especially in spring and summer when wild flowers seem to adorn every available patch of greenery.

From Laguna Hondera take a cairned path that zig-zags up the steep hillside south of the lake to reach a small col, where a large cairn marks the spot at which the eastern traverse path joins the east ridge of Mulhacén. Follow the path south as it contours around two wide bowls.

Snow can remain long into the summer in these **eastern bowls**, which have a wild and untamed feel to them. Many endemic plants are to be found in the *borreguiles* (high meadows) and alongside streams. Large herds of Spanish ibex frequently graze here.

Climbing up from Laguna Hondera to start the eastern traverse (Photo: Andrew Phillips)

The eastern traverse ends at some large cairns on the eastern side of a large plateau area at around 3080m. There are signs of an old road, which provides an easy option in mist. Cross the plateau to join the main path descending from Mulhacén.

At a corner of the road and junction of the Mulhacén path you will see 'Mulhacén' and '7 Lagunas' markers painted on a **rock**; at this point take a faint path south west and down some scree to cross the old trans-Sierra Nevada road before dropping down a shallow gully to a dirt road. Turn right to reach the **refuge**.

Alternative descent
A longer (by 1hr, 3km) but safer descent from the painted stone marker in mist or poor conditions is to continue down the main, well-cairned path to **Alto de Chorrillo**. From here a signposted dirt road leads to the refuge without difficulty.

ROUTE 9
The Púlpitos

Start/Finish	Refugio Poqueira
Distance	10km
Total ascent	670m
Grade	Moderate
Time	4hr 30min
Summits	Pico del Púlpito, El Púlpito
Water sources	Río Mulhacén, Río Seco, Laguna de las Cabras
Seasonal notes	Care is required in winter when descending into the valley of the Río Seco, as the slopes to the left steepen significantly.
Note	The Penebetica map shows both Pico del Púlpito and El Púlpito. On other maps, only El Púlpito is marked and Pico del Púlpito is named as 'Terreras Azules'.

This route is useful as a half-day or acclimatisation trip from the refuge. The Púlpitos are quiet peaks, rarely ascended as they don't reach the magical 3000m, but they nevertheless provide fine objectives for an easier day.

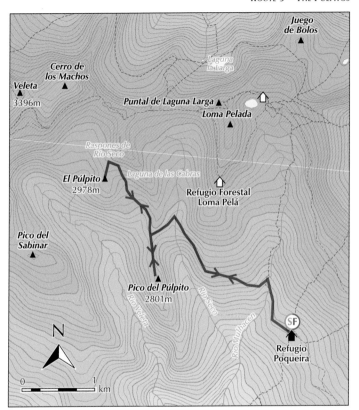

From the doorway of the refuge, Pico del Púlpito rises directly opposite. El Púlpito is hidden away to the right up a side-valley. Take the path that leads north west into the **Río Mulhacén**; cross the river and pick up a track opposite that takes a rising traverse across the hillside towards the valley of the Río Seco. As the valley comes into view the ground steepens noticeably and the descent towards the valley begins.

On reaching the **Río Seco**, cross the river and follow a faint track across the base of the jagged ridge of **Raspones de Río Seco**. The going is straightforward and soon the col is reached. Climb south along the ridge to reach the summit of **Pico del Púlpito** (2801m; 2hr, 3.5km) in 15min.

The north ridge of Pico del Púlpito (Photo: Felipe Nieto Conejero)

From the summit of Pico del Púlpito there are expansive **views** south to the Mediterranean Sea and north to the higher peaks comprising the main ridge of the Sierra Nevada.

Retrace your steps to the col and traverse into the valley north west and to the west of the Raspones de Río Seco ridge. This valley has a wild and remote feel to it, especially in winter conditions. There are a few faint tracks and the way forward is quite obvious. The peak of El Púlpito rises ahead and looks better than its sub-3000m height suggests.

Climb the valley between El Púlpito and Raspones to **Laguna de las Cabras**. Turn left and ascend steepening slopes to the summit ridge and hence to the summit of **El Púlpito** (2978m; 3hr, 5.5km).

Return the same way to the col and follow the outward path back to **Refugio Poqueira**.

WESTERN ALPUJARRAS

Following the old road towards Refugio Ventura, with Cerro del Caballo in the distance (Route 11)

This section covers the south west access to the Sierra Nevada from Soportújar (east) to Nigüelas (west). To reach the walks in this area it is often necessary to travel on dirt or forest tracks; for this reason the mountain walks tend to be much quieter and wilder. It is sometimes possible to go days without seeing another soul.

Both **Soportújar** and **Cañar** have some limited rental accommodation available. Although alongside the long-distance GR7 path, they can only be recommended to lovers of quiet and solitude!

Órgiva is the main market town of the Alpujarras and has a great range of accommodation options to suit all budgets and tastes. It has a very popular, bustling and lively Thursday market. The town is popular with the alternative community. There are some hotels, and lots of rental accommodation available throughout the year.

Lanjarón provides a convenient base for exploration both east and west. It has easy motorway access and is just 45min by car from both Granada and Capileira. It is a friendly and traditional Spanish spa town with a pleasant relaxed

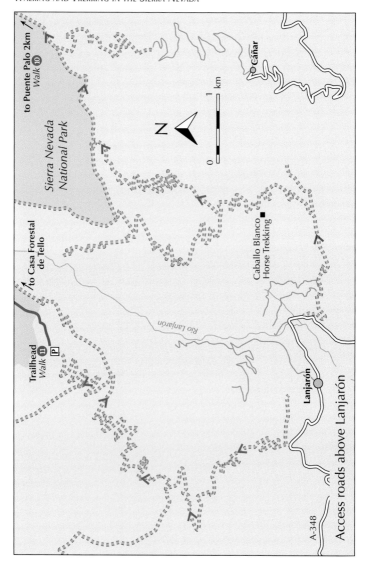

to Puente Palo 2km
Walk 10

Sierra Nevada
National Park

to Casa Forestal
de Tello

Trailhead
Walk 11 P

Cáñar

N

1 km
0

Caballo Blanco
Horse Trekking

Río Lanjarón

Lanjarón

A-348

Access roads above Lanjarón

atmosphere (except in January and February, when most hotels close and it becomes a ghost town). There are plenty of accommodation options, including the España, Alcadima, Castillo, Central and Nuevo Palas hotels. There are lots of villa and apartment rental properties available too. Tapas bars abound – in particular Bodega González, Bistro 31 and Casita de Papel. Lanjarón also has spa baths and an Arab castle, as well as a very good tourist office.

The Fiesta de San Juan, arguably the world's biggest water fight (*Carrera de Agua*), is held in Lanjarón towards the end of June – a uniquely Spanish experience celebrating the abundance of ham and water. It's a lot of fun if you don't mind getting wet! (It's important to book well in advance, however, if you're thinking of staying locally at that time.)

The **Lecrin valley** has superb views to Cerro de Caballo, and with good motorway and road connections it's within easy reach of Granada and the Alpujarras. The valley itself provides some good quiet winter walking and hiking tours away from the high Sierra Nevada. The town of Pinos del Valle is close to the motorway and has mainly guest house accommodation, such as Casa Molino. Bar Venecia provides much-needed sustenance after a hard day's walking!

Nigüelas and **Durcal** are both close to the Granada-Motril motorway and offer convenient access to Cerro de Caballo – although a 4WD vehicle is recommended for the dirt track above the town.

Getting to Lanjarón

Routes 10 and 11 are accessed from Lanjarón (650m), which is a 10min drive from the main A-44 motorway between Granada and Motril. The town provides access to the southern Sierra Nevada, including the 3000m peaks of Cerro del Caballo and Pico del Tajo de los Machos.

Getting to Puente Palo
(50min, 12km from Lanjarón)

Puente Palo is the start-point for Route 10. For much of the year it can be accessed by normal saloon cars, either along the route described below or via the Ermita Padre Eterno near Soportújar further to the east.

Leave Lanjarón to the east, and some 400m after crossing the bridge over the Río Lanjarón take a road on the left signposted 'Caballo Blanco'. This concrete road climbs the hillside and passes under an *acequia* (irrigation channel) bridge. Rough tracks are encountered at km3.

Keep zig-zagging upwards to a junction at km6. Here turn right (signed to Cañar), and at km10 (1690m) you'll meet another road. Turn right. The car park and recreation area at Puente Palo are another 2km distant.

Getting to the trailhead south of Peña Caballera
(1hr, 16.5km from Lanjarón)
The trailhead is the start-point for Route 11. At the western end of Lanjarón, go up a road on the right between Hotel Balneario and Bar Frenazo. The road deteriorates into a dirt track after a few kilometres. After 30min, at a junction of tracks, there are signposts for both Tello (right) and Ventura (left). Keep following the Ventura signs for another 15min.

At a high forest the track begins to trend eastwards into the Lanjarón valley and views of Cerrillo Redondo and Cerro de Caballo appear ahead. A chain across the track halts progress, and the car can be parked here. (Until 2014 the track took vehicles to within 15min of Refugio Ventura, but it is now closed to the public – meaning an additional hour's walk to reach the same point.)

Getting to Nigüelas
Route 12 is accessed from the village of Nigüelas, which lies just off the main A-44 motorway between Granada and Motril. A series of dirt tracks leads above the village – these are especially useful for access to the western Sierra Nevada.

Getting to Mirador de Rinconada de Nigüelas
(45min, 14.5km from Nigüelas; 4WD recommended)
The mirador is the start-point for Route 12. Although normal saloon cars are often seen on the access track outside of the winter months, much depends on the state of the dirt track at any given time. An alternative option is to use the local four-wheel drive taxi service (an eight-seat Land Rover) from Nigüelas: tel +34 696 710 769.

Make your way through the village and cross the river, then turn left. The rough track leads up the valley with impressive rock scenery for 2km before crossing a ford, after which there is a series of steep zig-zags before the road levels at Loma del Perro (1700m, 25min).

Continue up the Loma; the track circumvents the low hills until you emerge on a plateau just before Cortijos de Echevarría (1900m, 40min). At the junction, turn right. After 5min you'll reach the Mirador de Rinconada at a corner where the view into Rinconada de Nigüelas and Cerro del Caballo opens out.

ROUTE 10

Pico del Tajo de los Machos and Cerrillo Redondo

Start/Finish	Puente Palo recreation area
Distance	17.5km
Total ascent	1410m
Grade	Tough
Time	8hr 30min
Summits	Las Alegas, Pico del Tajo de los Machos, Cerrillo Redondo
Water sources	Río Chico
Seasonal notes	In winter this route could take two days, giving an opportunity to spend a night in the old Refugio Cebollar. After fresh snows the valley of the Río Chico will require snowshoes, and the ridge from Pico del Tajo de los Machos will be extremely icy – especially after strong winds – and is subject to cornicing.

For those who like their mountains tough, rugged, wild and unfrequented, this is a 'must-do' outing. A circular route full of interest, challenges and glorious scenery culminating in the ascent of a rarely visited 3000m peak.

From the recreation area take the forest track (often chained) ascending to the left (north east). Follow the twists and turns in this main forest track, ignoring all exits until at 2000m an overgrown track comes in from the right. Take this track, and after 50m there are signs of a previous landslip; soon afterwards, cross over a stream through a makeshift gate.

The track now rises in a gentle ascent on open hillside with the gorge of the Río Chico always to the right. Cross over the infant Río Chico at 2250m at a junction with **Barranco de Cortes** (2hr, 4km).

The **junction of the two rivers** is in a superb situation – possibly one of the finest places in the Sierras to sit and contemplate the meaning of life! In times of spate or spring snowmelt it can be difficult to cross.

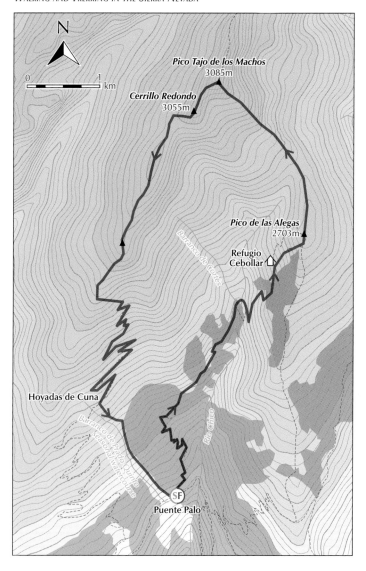

Ascending through the forests and hillsides towards the upper Río Chico

The toughest part of the day now follows as a 250m ascent to Refugio Cebollar is made. Follow the path east of the Río Chico crossing; it looks inviting but soon gets lost amid stones, boulders and overgrown shrubs. At some point a direct line for the prominent rocks at the top right-hand edge of the forest has to be made. These rocks are a good marker: just beyond them and at the top of the forest you rejoin a good track which leads easily to **Refugio Cebollar** (3hr, 5.5km).

The **refugio**, which sits on a small alpine-type plateau at 2500m, was built to house reforestation workers in the Franco era. It has a spring some 30m to the north that provides year-round cool, fresh water. The refuge itself is quite dilapidated but would provide emergency shelter.

Ascend directly on the steep slopes north east from the refuge, avoiding the low crags, to emerge near the summit of **Pico de Las Alegas** (2700m; 3hr 45min, 6km).

The entire onward route is visible from here, with the ridge on the right leading to Pico del Tajo de los Machos and then the connecting ridge to the left-hand peak of Cerrillo Redondo. To the north Mulhacén and the ridge to Veleta dominate **the scene**.

From the summit, a faint path drops steadily along the broad ridge northwards to a col. There are some fine bivouac sites around here to spend a night in the high mountains. The next section – an ascent of the south east ridge of Tajo de los Machos – is quite tough, being mainly pathless over stones and boulders. Keep to the ridge crest for the best views into the Toril valley to the right, and pass to the right of a substantial rock pinnacle near the top. From here the summit of **Pico del Tajo de los Machos** is just a few metres away (3085m; 5hr 30min, 9km). The view into the Lanjarón valley to the west opens up at this point, with the ridge between Tozal del Cartujo and the Cerro del Caballo rising behind.

It is possible to follow the ridge north from the summit to Refugio Elorrieta and the main ridge in one hour – a straightforward walk except for a rocky prominence halfway along which needs either climbing or avoiding to the left – but our route now lies south west along the broad ridge to the sub-peak of **Cerrillo Redondo** (3055m; 6hr, 7.5km), which you should reach 30min after the previous summit. Keep the escarpment edge on your left for the best views.

Heading south west from Cerrillo Redondo, follow the undulating ridge on faint tracks to a large cairn on the last major **summit** of the ridge at 2900m (7hr, 11.5km; also named on some older maps as Cerrillo Redondo). From here drop some 200m to the south west before taking an unmarked and pathless traverse to the east to the remnants of an old road at 2620m.

Winter view from Pico del Tajo de los Machos towards Cerro de Caballo

Follow this old road, cutting off the corners as and when necessary, to **Hoyadas de Cuna** (2280m) – the gully signifying the start of Barranco de Prado Quinto. This reaches the forest edge below and from there the firebreak is followed keeping the forest on the left. In winter this shallow gully makes a fast descent back to the start-point, but in summer conditions are more laborious. Either way it is a direct line and **Puente Palo** will be reached within an hour of the start of the *barranco* (gorge).

ROUTE 11

Ascent of Cerro del Caballo from the south

Start/Finish	Trailhead south of Peña Caballera
Alternative start	Near bridge over the Río Lanjarón, Lanjarón
Distance	19km; from Lanjarón: 34km
Total ascent	1060m; from Lanjarón: 2320m
Grade	Challenging; from Lanjarón: tough
Time	6hr 30min; from Lanjarón: 13hr 15min/2 days
Summits	Cerro de Caballo, Peña Caballera
Water sources	Laguna del Caballo, bowl south of ruins near Hoya del Zorro
Seasonal notes	In winter the south west ridge in its entirety might be a better option rather than the flanking paths described below, and there is normally heavy icing on the slopes north and east of the summit. In summer, especially if starting from Lanjarón and splitting the walk across two days, carry plenty of water.

A long ascent of Europe's most southerly 3000m peak, ascending high above the Lanjarón valley and then descending with extensive views towards the western mountains and plains.

The old way to climb Cerro del Caballo, from the town of Lanjarón itself, is described as an alternative here – but this is a tough climb involving over 2300m of ascent and is better split into a two-day ascent, camping at Refugio Ventura – or even higher.

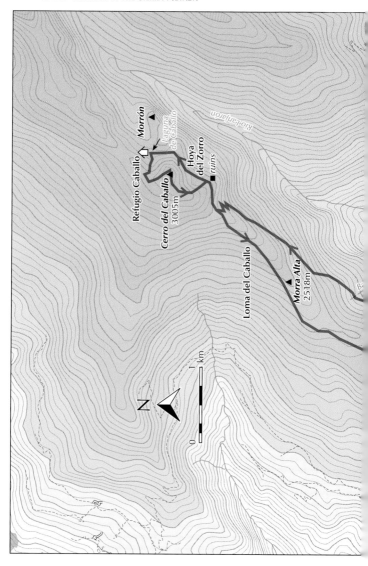

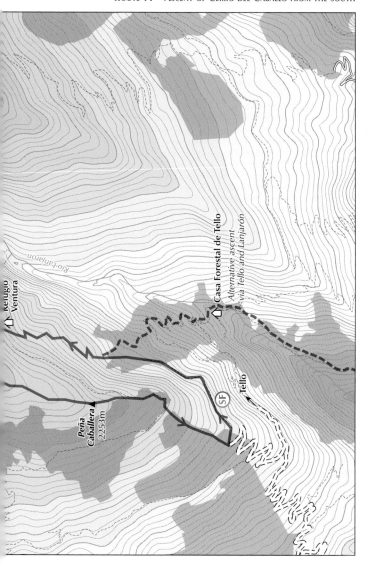

Follow the road into the Lanjarón valley high above the river. The old road can be used in its entirety, although some of its longer zig-zags are cut short by linking paths. After 1hr the old car park below **Refugio Ventura** is reached. Take the good path that leads in 15min to the old refuge (1hr 15min, 4km).

Alternative ascent from Lanjarón to Refugio Ventura

From just east of the bridge over the Río Lanjarón on the eastern side of town, take the 'Camino de las Sierras' – a well-marked drovers' trail. This rises and traverses the eastern side of the Lanjarón valley, until just below the ruined buildings of **Casa Forestal de Tello** (3hr, 5.5km).

Behind Tello, follow tracks that make their way relentlessly uphill in a series of bends and zig-zags to join the main ascent route some 2km south of **Refugio Ventura** (5hr 30min, 11.5km).

The path continues behind the refuge and rises steeply to an irrigation channel. Turn right and follow the channel for 1km until you cross the gorge of **Barranco Intestral**, then leave the channel for a path on the left which rises up on the south east side of a plantation.

The track continues rising south east of the main ridge line (**Loma del Caballo**) and becomes rockier as height is gained. Reach an open bowl. There is normally running water here until late summer. Turn left up a steep track to the head of the bowl at 2700m; the path now leads round the valley head to reach old **ruins** south of the summit at 2830m (2hr 45min, 8km). The southern aspect of Cerro del Caballo lies in front of you: the following route will take you round to the right to ascend the summit from the north.

There's no obvious reason why the peak is named the Cerro de Caballo (**'Peak of the Horse'**) – unless you're on the mountain ridge south of Cerrillo Redondo to its east. In certain winter conditions the snow-filled ledges and gullies of the eastern face of Cerro de Caballo can resemble a horse's head and bridle.

A small descent north of the ruins leads easily into the bowl of the **Hoya del Zorro** and around to a superb vantage point at 2885m.

The viewpoint offers panoramic **vistas**. Ahead lies the long upper valley of the Río Lanjarón; to the left is the long, high ridge between Cerro del Caballo, Tajos Altos and Pico de Tozal del Cartujo; and to the right of the valley is the less impressive ridge to Pico del Tajos de los Machos.

The track leads north west from here in 15min to **Refugio del Caballo** (3hr 15min, 9km), which is situated in a very pleasant spot with the tranquil waters of Laguna del Caballo just behind. This makes a good camping place if preferred to the refuge.

Take a steep ascent to the col north of the summit and then follow the escarpment edge to the summit of **Cerro de Caballo** (3011m; 4hr, 10km), which you should reach some 45min after the refuge. The view from the most southerly 3000m peak in Europe is extensive, but it's the mountains of the Sierra Nevada to the north east that hold the eye.

Take faint tracks leading south west from the summit and around the escarpment edge to arrive back at the ruins in 30min. Return round the head of the bowl, but where the ascent track turns to drop down to the left, branch off on a faint track over a small col to the south west. The track improves as it descends and rapid progress will be made, always to the north west of the main ridge of the Loma del Caballo.

The track passes west of **Morra Alta** (2518m) then widens and is easily followed over **Peña Caballera** (2253m) to join a 4WD track heading south. As the road moves around to the west, take the first forest break leading steeply down to join the main 4WD. Turn left and return to the car in a further 10min.

From the summit looking north past Laguna del Caballo to Tajos Altos, Tozal del Cartujo and Veleta (Photo: Javier Aguirrebengoa)

ROUTE 12

Ascent of Cerro del Caballo via los Tres Mojones

Start/Finish	Mirador de Rinconada, above Nigüelas
Distance	11.5km
Total ascent	900m
Grade	Challenging
Time	5hr 15min
Summits	Cerro de Caballo
Water sources	None except at Laguna del Caballo
Seasonal notes	In winter the western flanks of Cerro del Caballo get blasted by the prevailing winds from the south west and hence frequently expose the snow to bare ice.

A circular route and the quickest way to ascend Europe's most southerly 3000m peak – although the state of the access track might deter some (see 'Getting to Mirador de Rinconada de Nigüelas', above).

View to Refugio del Caballo from the south east

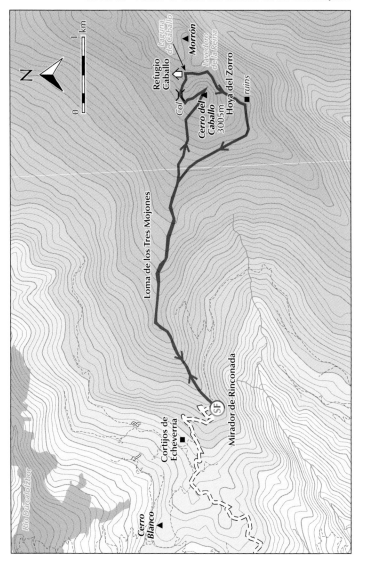

Take the path opposite the mirador that leads through a small plantation of pines and ascends steadily north east to join the **Loma de los Tres Mojones**. This broad ridge turns towards the east; follow the faint path rising towards Cerro del Caballo ahead.

Close to the summit the main path from the col to the north joins from the left. Follow this to the summit of **Cerro del Caballo** (3051m; 2hr 30min, 5km), enjoying the spectacular views down to the lake and refuge to the left.

Descend the same way initially until a direct route north west on a good path can be taken to the col. From the **col**, drop east down the steep hillside directly to Laguna del Caballo, which is nestled in the cirque below with the **refuge** just beyond (3hr, 5.5km).

> If time permits, the prominent peak beyond the lake, **Morrón** (2868m), is well worth a visit for the sensational vistas northwards down the length of the Lanjarón valley. Allow 45min for the return trip from the refuge.

From the refuge take a path traversing south east across the head of the bowl containing the small lake of Lavadero de la Reina; this continues south west via Hoya del Zorro to reach some **ruins** at 2830m (3hr 30min, 6.5km).

Continue past the ruins and down towards the pass beyond. The next section of the route is pathless as you contour around the south west side of the peak, making a slow descending traverse over rough stony ground at or about the 2800m level to rejoin **Loma de los Tres Mojones**. Rejoin the outward route and follow it back to the start-point at **Mirador de Rinconada**.

DÍLAR VALLEY

The ridges of Alayos del Dílar and Trevenque from Silleta de Padul (Photo: Kiersten Rowland) (Route 13)

The Dílar valley gives access to some relatively unknown walking south of the Cumbres Verdes range, and in particular the river valley leading to the spectacular Los Alayos de Dílar ridge. The lush greenery of the upper Dílar valley contrasts with the stark aridness of the ridge itself. By contrast the terrain between this and Silleta de Padul is wooded hill country, giving pleasant and straightforward walking trails with good views over the Vega de Granada to the west.

In the main summer months the walks in this region may well be too hot to consider, due to the relatively low altitude of the mountains.

The town of Dílar itself has Hotel Zerbinetta very close to the Silleta de Padul trailhead, and it also has some guest house accommodation available, but the town is so close to the Granada motorway network that most visitors will choose to stay in Granada. The Merendero los Alayos restaurant has a good reputation and is conveniently situated by the car park for the walk to Alayos de Dílar ridge.

Getting to Ermita de Nuestra Señora de las Nieves, Dílar

Ermita Nueva is the start-point for Route 13. Leave the main autovía, Sierra Nevada-Costa Tropical (A44), at km139 and follow the GR-3301 through the town of Otura to Dílar (5km, 10min). Once there, look out for signs pointing to the 'Ermita'.

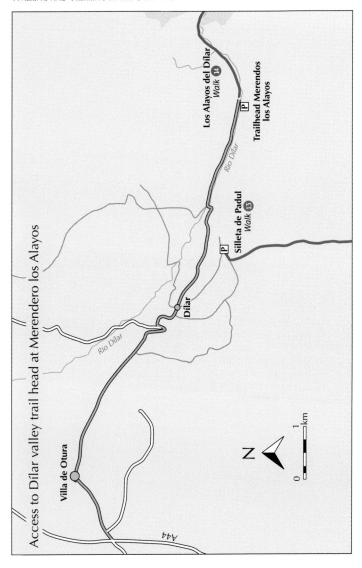

Access to Dílar valley trail head at Merendero los Alayos

Los Alayos del Dílar *Walk 14*

Trailhead Merendos los Alayos

Silleta de Padul *Walk 15*

Río Dílar

Dílar

Río Dílar

Villa de Otura

A44

N

0 1 km

After entering Dílar carry on up the hill and turn right, following the one-way system. There is a bus stop on the right. Continue along the road and take the right fork (signposted 'Rio Dílar'). At a stop sign turn right up the hill to a T-junction. Turn immediately right and then left onto Calle Av. Emelio Muñoz. This road leads to the Ermita on the right. At the crossroads 200m beyond is a parking area (7km, 15min from autovía).

Getting to Dílar trailhead
The trailhead is the start-point for Route 14. Leave the main autovía Sierra Nevada-Costa Tropical (A44) at km139 and follow the GR-3301 through the town of Otura to Dílar (5km, 10min). Continue through Dílar on the Carretera Fabrica de la Luz (SE-9) until it crosses over the Río Dílar at a bridge. Turn immediately right and follow this road to the car park and trailhead by the Merendero los Alayos restaurant (10km, 25min from autovía).

ROUTE 13
Silleta de Padul

Start/Finish	Ermita de Nuestra Señora de las Nieves, Dílar
Distance	13km
Total ascent	570m
Grade	Moderate
Time	5hr 30min
Summits	Silleta de Padul
Water sources	Spring water available from a fountain a short way beyond Ermita Vieja
Seasonal notes	It's very rare for this route to be snow-covered for more than a few days during the winter months. Generally too hot during the summer months, although the trees may provide some welcome shade and relief.

Silleta de Padul is at the very western end of the Sierra Nevada. It commands a spectacular 360-degree view and is well worth the effort of the steep ascent through pine forests to its summit. After traversing low ridges to the east a return is made north west through forests back to the start.

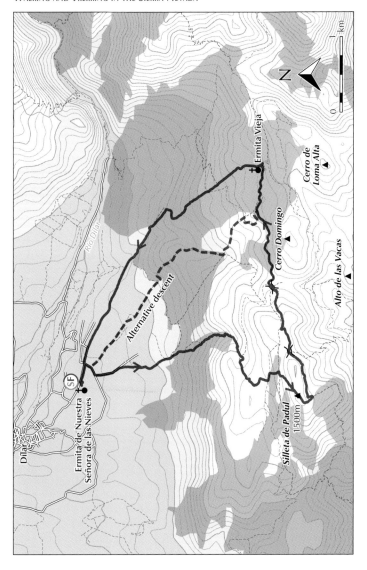

The path east from the summit, with the white snows of the Sierra Nevada looming ahead (Photo: Kiersten Rowland)

From the crossroads, follow the tarmac road south west – it quickly changes to a cobbled road after 100m. Take the dirt track immediately on the left which ascends slowly through olive groves to pass right of a rectangular water storage *alberca*.

The path, directly ahead, rises through sparsely populated pine forests to join a shallow valley which trends round to the south west to emerge at a level cultivated field. Silleta de Padul is the obvious peak directly ahead. Cross the field and turn left at the land rover track, then after 100m turn right and ascend to a small olive grove which is crossed to join a path signposted 'La Silleta' and 'Ermita Vieja'. This leads easily to a col just east of the summit (2hr, 5km).

Take the short detour to the west to visit the summit of **Silleta de Padul** (1500m) and enjoy the fantastic view back east to the Sierra Nevada, with Veleta, Tozal del Cartujo and Cerro de Caballo being the prominent peaks. Return to the col and take the well-marked path descending south west. This path would eventually lead down to the town of Padul, so it's important to look for a path diverging off to the left, marked by a post, some 300m after leaving the col.

Our path traverses north east below Silleta de Padul, whose slopes are now on the left. At another **col**, east of the peak, superb views to both Trevenque and the Los Alayos de Dílar ridge open up to the north. Continue south of the small ridge line until a forest track is met.

Alternative descent

Some 700m short of Ermita Vieja it is possible to shorten the walk by an hour by taking the track marked 'Ermita Nueva' and, after a further 1km, taking care to leave this track on another path going to the right. This takes you back to **Ermita de Nuestra Señora de las Nieves** and the start.

Turn right onto the forest track, following signs to Ermita Vieja, which you reach after passing through a range of small forested hillsides and valleys (3hr 30min, 9km).

> **Ermita Vieja** is a special place for locals who come up here on pilgrimage on 5 August for the Festividad de Nuestra Señora de las Nieves – the patron of Dílar. The Ermita also acts as a fire lookout station during the long, hot summer months.

> Just past the Ermita is a path to the left which descends the firebreak: this is your return back to the start-point. Lower down, make sure to keep left of the ruined wall alongside the firebreak to ensure the correct path is taken. On leaving the tree line it might look a long way back, but it's a simple and relatively speedy return to **Ermita de Nuestra Señora de las Nieves**.

The long track leading back to the town of Dílar (Photo: Kiersten Rowland)

ROUTE 14
Integral de los Alayos

Start/Finish	Car park at Merendero los Alayos restaurant, Dílar valley trailhead
Distance	20km
Total ascent	980m
Grade	Tough
Time	7hr 30min
Summits	Corazón de la Sandia
Water sources	Only in the Río Dílar at the start and end
Seasonal notes	It isn't often this range is white, but when it is it will consist of powder snow, rarely consolidating, but giving a rewarding winter excursion. Between mid June and mid September it is usually far too hot to do this walk.

The long ridge bordering the southern side of the Río Dílar valley takes you into a Wild West-type landscape that contrasts greatly with the lushness of the Río Dílar. The first task is to get to Collado del Pino at the far eastern side of the main Alayos ridge. The ridge itself can be followed in its entirety by those with a head for heights and loads of surplus energy; otherwise there's a good but narrow path just below the actual ridge crest.

The ridge has many summits but the best is possibly Corazón de la Sandía. This peak is 1877m high and involves a somewhat exposed scramble to reach its rocky top. This whole area has thick green forest on one side of the ridge crest and arid badlands on the other, making it an interesting day out.

The path goes east from the car park along the northern banks of the **Río Dílar** and into the obvious narrowing gorge ahead. Soon pass a recreation area with picnic tables, and follow the path as it crosses the river numerous times during the ascent upstream.

Eventually the river is left behind. Take the forest track, and leave this soon after crossing the Canal de la Espartera to take a good path leading in 5min to **Toma del Canal** (2hr, 8km).

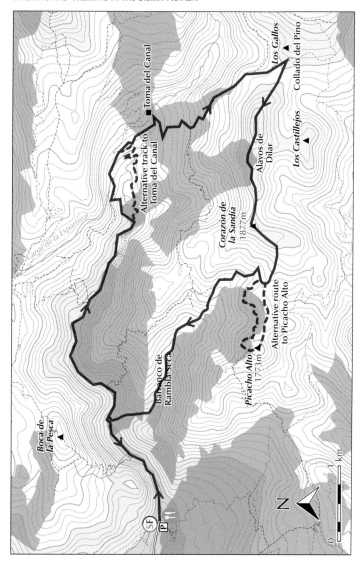

Looking down on the initial narrow section of the Río Dílar valley

Just below Toma del Canal the path crosses the Río Dílar again and makes its way uphill through a forested area that climbs up to the col, **Collado del Pino** (1800m), and the start of the **Alayos de Dílar** ridge (4hr, 11km). The arid nature of this area now becomes evident with a certain 'Wild West' flavour to the scenery. Climb easily to the first point on the ridge at 1975m.

The ridge ahead looks interesting and suggests that there may be good scrambling along its crest. The reality, however, is disappointing. The crest is a mix of shrub and rocky boulders, and although it gives good views it is unsatisfactory as a walking route – better to follow the faint track south of the ridge line.

At the western end of the Los Alayos ridge is the finest peak on the ridge: a short scramble on the south west side is required to reach the sharp summit of the strangely named peak of **Corazón de la Sandía** ('Heart of the Watermelon', 1877m, 5hr 30min, 14km).

From here a path leads quickly south west to a minor summit on the ridge, marked only as '1868m' on the map. From there turn west and drop down a short, steep slope to a small col (6hr). Ahead lies the ridge rising to Picacho Alto. Descend rough slopes northwards for a short distance to join another more distinct path. Continue continue descending into the valley bottom.

The spectacular Corazón de la Sandía from the ridge to the south west

Optional ascent of Picacho Alto
An ascent of Picacho Alto will take around 45min and add 100m of ascent. From
the col east of Picacho Alto, head west over a series of undulating minor summits
to reach **Picacho Alto** (1773m). Return to join the main route again just north of
the col by following a decent path crossing Picacho Alto's northern slopes.

A good path drops into the complex series of dry *barrancos* (canyons) and *ramblas*
(streambeds) that converge into **Barranco de Rambla Seca**. This is a fascinating
dry riverbed.

> The **Barranco de Rambla Seca** (literally, 'Ravine of the Dry Creek') is well
> named. A narrow valley hemmed in by hillsides and rock walls, in times of
> flash flooding it must be an incredible sight to behold.

Towards the end of the valley, steep rock walls converge and narrow, and
then the valley opens out again and you cross the **Río Dílar** to rejoin the outward
route just a few hundred metres from the restaurant car park.

CUMBRES VERDES

From the slopes of Cerro Gordo there are stunning views to the east (Photo: Andrew Phillips) (Route 18)

The Cumbres Verdes ('Green Peaks') range lies very close to the city of Granada, only 15 minutes by car from the main Circunvalación ring road. The mountains are divided into a series of sub-ranges that give really interesting and entertaining circular walks either side of the Arroyo del Huenes river valley. One of the endearing features here is the contrast between the lush green pine-forested hillsides and valleys and the stark, arid badland scenery that would not look out of place in a Spaghetti Western movie.

Given the easy access, the Cumbres Verdes are well known to Granadinos. In spite of this the walking is quiet and unspoilt – especially during the week – and has a certain attraction that is lacking in the higher and wilder Sierra Nevada, with the contrasting scenery affording interesting and enjoyable views.

In the main summer months the walks in this region may well be far too hot due to the relatively low altitude of the mountains – although a pre-dawn start will be rewarded. By contrast the walks here can make useful alternatives for poor-weather days in the higher mountains of the Sierra Nevada.

The upmarket village of **Cumbres Verdes** lies close to most of the trailheads in this area. There are a few hotels and apartments to choose from, as well as bars and restaurants.

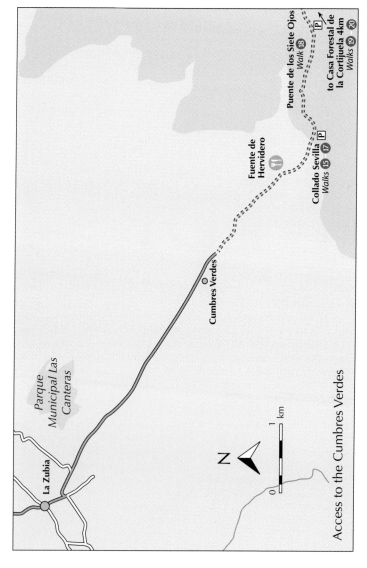

Puente de los Siete Ojos *Walk* 18

P

to Casa Forestal de
la Cortijuela 4km
Walks 19 - 20

Fuente de
Hervidero

Collado Sevilla *Walks* 15 17

P

Cumbres Verdes

Parque
Municipal Las
Canteras

La Zubia

N

0   1 km

Access to the Cumbres Verdes

La Zubia, just a few minutes' drive to the north west, is really just a sprawling suburb of Granada – and in fact most visitors to the area will choose to stay in the city of Granada itself with its bustling nightlife, superb tapas bars, and of course historical buildings such as the Alhambra Palace or the Cathedral.

Getting to Collado Sevilla from Granada

Collado Sevilla is the start-point for Routes 15, 16 and 17. The start-point for Route 18 is just 2km further along the road from Collado Sevilla (though cars may be left at the point where the return route joins the main dirt road if the 1km of road to Puente de Siete Ojos proves too rough for saloon cars).

Leave the autovía Sierra Nevada A-395 at km2, signposted La Zubia. At the town, continue straight on to a small roundabout. Take the fourth exit, heading back down the hill for 30m. Turn right and at the next junction turn right again onto Calle Cruz de San Antón, which leads easily to Carretera Cumbres Verdes. Continue up the hill for 4km to a junction next to the Restaurante La Guitarra, just outside the small village of Cumbres Verdes; turn left onto a forest track (normally suitable for saloon cars) and follow this, keeping right at Fuente de Hervidero to reach the car park at Collado Sevilla (20min, 12km from the autovía).

Getting to Casa Forestal de la Cortijuela

The Casa is the start-point for Routes 19 and 20. Access is via the main road through La Zubia and Cumbres Verdes to Collado Sevilla (see above). From there continue left, ignoring the entry to the Collado Sevilla car park, before dropping into the valley of Arroyo de Huenes. About 4km past the bridge at Puente de Siete Ojos, the Casa Forestal de la Cortijuela is reached. (Note that in 2017 the dirt road immediately before Puente de Siete Ojos was deteriorating badly and becoming difficult for saloon cars.)

ROUTE 15
Boca de la Pesca

Start/Finish	Car park, Collado Sevilla
Distance	8km
Total ascent	330m
Grade	Leisurely
Time	2hr 30min
Summits	Cerro de las Pipas, Boca de la Pesca
Water sources	None
Seasonal notes	It is normally too hot in July and August for comfortable walking.

A short half-day or evening stroll to the prominent peak of Boca de la Pesca, which guards the entrance to the Dílar valley and gives fine and distant views across to the mountains of the Cumbres Verdes, Sierra Nevada and the plains west of Granada.

This circular route starts and is described from Collado Sevilla, but the walk could also be started from La Fuente del Hervidero where there is even more ample parking.

From Cortijo Sevilla follow the dirt track south west (marked 'Haza Larguilla') past a few small houses and holiday homes. A fine viewpoint is passed on the left, and 300m later the track narrows and becomes a mountain path which heads west over the small peak of **Cerro de las Pipas** (1428m) to a junction of paths.

Turn left (the right-hand path only leads on to join with the descent route!) and ascend on a good zig-zag path, eventually emerging from the trees to reach the fire observation building on top of **Boca de la Pesca** (1564m; 1hr 15min, 3km). The name means 'mouth of the fish' – due to the peak's supposed resemblance to a fish head when seen from the north east.

This is quite a viewpoint. There are **vistas** of Trevenque and Alayos de Dílar, with the ever-present stunning backdrop of the Sierra Nevada – especially beautiful when covered in sparkling winter snows. To the west, the plains around Granada seemingly stretch on forever. The southern slopes drop steeply into the Dílar gorge, and the Espartera Channel (a major and arduous

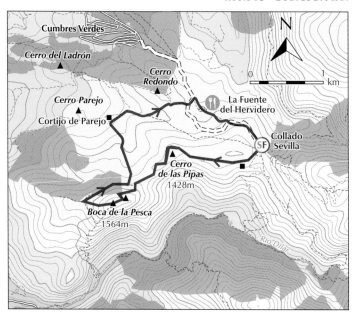

The Dílar valley shrouded in cloud, with Boca de la Pesca on the right

feat of engineering) can be seen dropping steeply into the depths of the Dílar valley gorge below.

The slightly higher **eastern peak** is a short but worthwhile 5min walk away. Return the same way to the fire observation point. From here descend west down a wide firebreak downhill to reach a junction with a path just above a small irrigation channel. Turn right here and continue traversing alongside the north western slopes.

On emerging from the trees, ignore the initial path and take the second (better) marked trail some 150m further on. After a further 1km, pass right of the buildings of **Cortijo de Parejo**, then turn right after another 150m onto a path. Some 300m later take a path on the left that rises steeply to cross over a hill. Below you will see the buildings at La Fuente del Hervidero, which can be reached by turning right and skirting the fields before dropping down to the road. Take a path that emerges from the south east end of the car park and leads easily back to the start-point at **Collado Sevilla**.

ROUTE 16
Trevenque via Cuerda del Trevenque

Start/Finish	Car park, Collado Sevilla
Distance	10km
Total ascent	670m
Grade	Moderate
Time	4hr
Summits	Trevenque
Water sources	None
Seasonal notes	It is normally too hot in July and August for comfortable walking. Any winter snows won't normally last long enough to consolidate, but after fresh powder snow the ascent is a superb experience.

The isolated peak of Trevenque (2079m) may not be the highest around, but without doubt it is one of the finest summits contained within this guide. Its classic mountain shape offers superb routes to a sharp summit with superlative views. A mountain ascent that should be on every visitor's tick list!

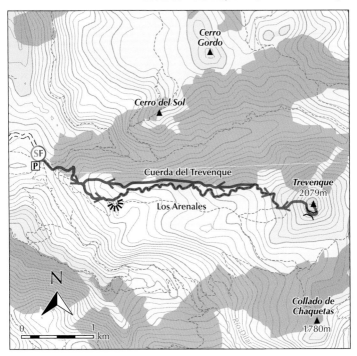

From the car park at Collado Sevilla, go east on the well-marked path past the noticeboard. After 200m turn left, and at the first corner take the narrow path ascending through low shrub and trees. This emerges onto a crest and into an area of arid badlands, which you traverse directly to a **mirador** (viewpoint) (30min, 1.5km).

> The mirador has an information board (in Spanish only) detailing the geological and ecological history of **Los 'arenales' del Trevenque**. It explains that the area was formed in the Middle and Upper Triassic ages (up to 240 million years ago), and that these are semi-arid sandy lanscapes where any living organism has had to adapt to the semi-desert ecosystem. Temperatures here can fluctuate tens of degrees between day and night, with extremes consisting of both high summer heat and mid-winter ice and snow. This situation means unique and endangered species.

131

Descending from the summit after fresh overnight powder snow

Turn left and follow the dirt track easily as it contours round the left-hand side of the valley. To the right are the arid badlands known as Las Arenales ('the sands'). (Just above and left of the road is the Cuerda del Trevenque – the route to be taken for the return journey.) When the dirt track meets the main mass of the mountain, take the path trending off to the left, which rises gently and heads directly for the peak ahead.

The way is obvious up the scree slope beyond; then continue on the path as it hugs the southern side of the jagged rocky west ridge and the basin beyond to emerge at a small col. Here a view to the western ridges of the Sierra Nevada opens out. Despite the steepness of the surrounding terrain, no hands are required and there is no scrambling involved.

Pass through the col, turn left and go northwards to climb up a short step to reach the airy summit of **Trevenque** (2079m; 2hr 15min, 5km).

Take care on the initial descent after the summit rocks as another path leads off to the south east, to Collado de Trevenque. The correct descent is to the right, returning to the small **col** south west of the summit area.

Retrace your steps to the junction with the dirt road, but instead of the road take the switchback ridge (**Cuerda del Trevenque**) that leads back to the start. Don't be tempted by the easy road to its left – the ridge is the infinitely better alternative. At times it comes down to meet the dirt road but the most enjoyable walking with the best views is always on the crest.

Eventually the path merges with the main path just a few hundred metres from the finish; turn right and follow this back to the car park.

ROUTE 17
Circuit of Trevenque and Dílar valley

Start/Finish	Car park, Collado Sevilla
Distance	12km; omitting ascent of Trevenque: 9.5km
Total ascent	900m; omitting ascent of Trevenque: 490m
Grade	Moderate
Time	5hr 30min; omitting ascent of Trevenque: 4hr 30min
Summits	Trevenque
Water sources	Springs at the head of Barranco de Aguas Blanquillas and at Refugio Forestal de Rosales
Seasonal notes	It is normally too hot in July and August for comfortable walking. On the rare days that winter conditions exist, the initial descent from the summit to Collado del Trevenque will require care.

A circular walk of contrasts and delights, this is another of the 'not-to-be-missed' walks in the Cumbres Verdes. The arid dryness of the rocky peak of Trevenque and Las Arenales contrast greatly with the green lushness of the upper Dílar valley and gorge. The walk is full of twists, turns and differing vistas, making it one of the most interesting walks in this book.

From the large car park at Collado Sevilla there are a couple of options to get to the *mirador* (viewpoint) overlooking Trevenque and the valley of Las Arenales. The first and most direct line takes maximum advantage of the amazing semi-desert badlands scenery: head south east and after 200m turn left along the wide track, then at the first corner take the narrow path ascending through low shrub and trees. This emerges onto a crest and into an area of arid badlands, which you traverse directly to the **mirador** and information board (30min, 1.5km).

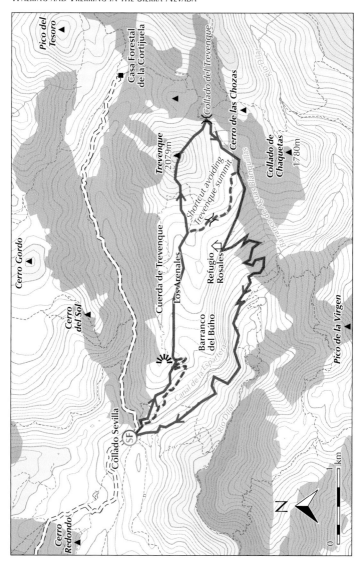

There are some great **views** on the ascent to the mirador – especially to the Los Alayos de Dílar ridge, the depths of the Dílar valley gorge and back to Boca de la Pesca.

Alternative route to the mirador
The alternative route to the mirador is straightforward but is 0.5km longer than the main route and will take around 15min longer. Follow the dirt track that ascends south east from the car park; a couple of long zig-zags bends lead to the **mirador** and information board.

Take a path behind the information board that drops into the valley beyond, and follow this dry valley as it twists and turns, trending eastwards with the constant vista of the peak ahead. Near the end of the valley the path splits and again you have two options. To include Trevenque in your route, take the left-hand path which climbs the low ridge, aiming directly for the peak itself. It is a good track but there are sections that are steep and loose.

Alternative route to Refugio Forestal de Rosales omitting Trevenque
The right-hand path cuts through the **pass** and goes quickly through mixed forest on a very good path to the forest road. On meeting the forest road, turn right and hence to **Refugio Forestal de Rosales**, where the main route is rejoined.

The steep and quite loose upper section after leaving the summit of Trevenque

135

The mountainside path winds its way into Barranco del Búho

After 600m and 130m ascent a dirt track joins from the left and the path steepens. The way is obvious. The path climbs south of the jagged rocky ridge and up into a broad shallow gully, aiming for a col right of the summit; despite the steepness of the surrounding terrain, no hands are required and there is no scrambling involved.

Nearing the summit, thread through a small col and a view of the western ridges of the Sierra Nevada opens out. The path turns north and in a few minutes reaches the summit area. Climb up a short step to reach the airy summit of **Trevenque** (2079m; 2hr 15min, 4km).

> The peak of **Trevenque** from any angle looks like a mountain should. It's conical and steep-sided, without any adjoining ridges. The airy summit gives good views in all directions but especially towards the higher peaks of the Sierra Nevada to the east.

Retrace steps from the summit for a few minutes, and at the junction of paths with the Cuerda del Trevenque descent route continue down the path to the south east. Far below and amid all the chaotic waste of arid badlands lies the next objective – Collado del Trevenque, a col at the base of the mountain where the forest road joins. The initial descent is on a good path but it's steep and loose, and appropriate care should be taken. On the descent, look out for the dry valley to the right of the col.

On reaching **Collado del Trevenque** (3hr, 5km), turn right. This is a fascinating area that would not be out of place in a Wild West movie. The dry valley (really the upper Barranco de Aguas Blanquillas) narrows, trees start to appear and then all of a sudden everything changes and you enter a lush green forested area. (It is here that the spring of Barranco de Aquas Blanquillas emerges from the ground – hence the dramatically changing vegetation.) The path leads to a forest road and a junction with the alternative path leading from the pass at Las Arenales.

Follow the pleasant forest road, which trends slightly downhill for 1km, to the delightful **Refugio Forestal de Rosales** (4hr, 7km; normally closed). A magnificent vista opens up here of the Dílar gorge and the ridge of Los Alayos beyond. A few metres east of the refuge is a refreshing spring.

> **Refugio Forestal de Rosales** is a pleasant place to take a break. There is good drinking water from the spring and a magnificent view across to the Alayos de Dílar ridge. Very conveniently, all the peaks are marked on a panoramic information board supplied by the Natural Park/Junta de Andalucía.

Continue down the forest road in a series of zig-zags to a bend below the Canal de la Espartera (1350m), then take a path to the right. This path remains high above the Dílar valley as it winds its way initially west then north west around the gorge of Barranco del Búho to gently rise up and return to the start-point at **Collado Sevilla**.

ROUTE 18
The Cerro Huenes group

Start/Finish	Puente de los Siete Ojos
Distance	11km
Total ascent	580m
Grade	Moderate
Time	5hr
Summits	Cerro del Sol, Pico de la Carne, Cerro Gordo, Cerro de las Minas, Cerro Huenes
Water sources	Fuente Fría, north of Cerro Huenes
Seasonal notes	It is normally too hot in July and August for comfortable walking. It's rare in winter to find snow here, and when it does snow it will be powder that disappears rapidly.

The Cerro Huenes group is in the northern Cumbres Verdes and is separated from the Trevenque range by the deep valley of Arroyo de Huenes. The mountains lie edged around a high plateau area. This route provides pleasant hiking on generally good trails over numerous mountains, returning through forested hillsides to the start.

Cross the *puente* (bridge) and take the path ascending over the minor summit of **Cerro del Sol** and onto the first peak, **Pico de la Carne** (1809m; 1hr, 1.5km). Although the hillsides here are steep, the path is well-graded and the summit is easily reached in 1hr – either via a short, easy scramble on the right of the summit rocks or by a flanking path to the left. There are superb views back to Trevenque and the Sierra Nevada from the summit.

Continue north on the path towards the next objective, **Cerro Gordo** (1809m; 1hr 30min, 2.5km), which lies 30min/1km away to the north east. From there a quick descent north west followed by a short climb brings you to **Cerro de las Minas** (1851m) in another 30min.

The reigning peak, **Cerro Huenes** (1882m; 2hr 30min, 4km), lies 1km to the north west across a flat plateau (Llanada del Chopo) area; the going is quick and easy, aided by numerous goat tracks all heading in a similar direction.

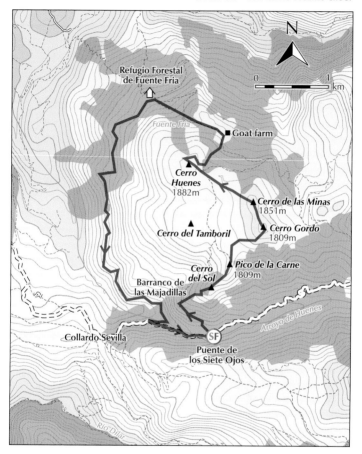

A short stroll to the south west from Llanada del Chopo would allow peak-baggers to claim the summit of **Cerro de Tamboril** (1773m), but a return must be made the same way.

The character of the walk changes as the route enters the forest east of Cerro Huenes. Take the good path, easily found, that descends north east through the forest to join a forest road. Turn left and follow this past a **goat farm** on the right.

Descending Cerro de las Minas en route to Cerro Huenes (Photo: Andrew Phillips)

After a further 1km, at a sharp right-hand bend in the road, is the spring at **Fuente Fría**. At this same bend take a path that leaves the forest road and descends to the ruins at **Refugio Forestal de Fuente Fría** (3hr 15min, 6km).

A good path (signposted) now leads round the western flanks of Cerro Huenes and Cerro del Tamboril, in and out of small *barrancos* (gorges), steadily losing height. After crossing **Barranco de las Majadillas**, cross the Arroyo de Huenes river and rejoin the main road. Turn left and walk up the road for 1km to the start-point at **Puente de los Siete Ojos**.

ROUTE 19
Pico del Tesoro and Cerro del Cocón

Start/Finish	Casa Forestal de la Cortijuela
Distance	8km
Total ascent	350m
Grade	Moderate
Time	3hr 30min
Summits	Pico del Tesoro, Cerro del Cocón
Water sources	Spring at Casa Forestal de la Cortijuela
Seasonal notes	It is normally too hot in July and August for comfortable walking. Winter snows don't normally last long enough to consolidate, but after fresh powder snow the area is delightful.

The wooded hillsides and arid hills north of the road approaching Casa Forestal de la Cortijuela provide an exceptionally beautiful walk with superb views. The route described here forms a figure-of-eight loop, ascending the rough peaks of Pico del Tesoro and Cerro del Cocón, and is perfect for a half-day excursion from Granada.

La Cortijuela Botanical Garden, next to the Casa Forestal, is part of the Andalucian network of botanical gardens, located in an area of extreme ecological value. The purpose of these gardens is to collect, catalogue, research and ultimately protect the threatened plants. Around 400 different types can be seen, including many endemic species, covering a wide range of environments.

It is free to visit and opens Tuesday to Sunday between 10am and 4pm. Due to the altitude, the gardens are closed between November and February. There are 2.5km of well laid-out trails involving a 100m height gain. Vulnerable plants or those in danger of extinction are clearly identified.

From the Casa, take the path behind the spring, signposted 'San Jeronimo', that rises gently north east through wooded hillsides to the col, **Collado de Matas Verdes** (45min 1.5km). A view towards Veleta, its San Francisco ridge and Loma del Dílar coming down from the ski resort come into view as you leave the tree line.

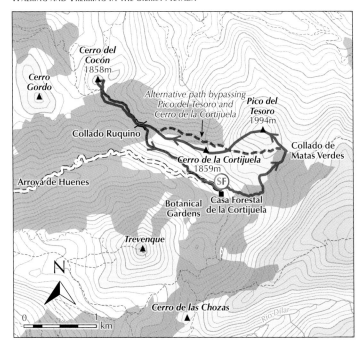

The path to Collado de Matas Verdes is actually part of the long-distance **Sulayr GR240** (Route 33) that encircles the Sierra Nevada and is well supplied with marker posts.

Pico del Tesoro is the obvious peak lying a short distance north west of the col. The slopes leading up to the peak are mainly pathless but there are vague indications left by ibex or goat herds of the easiest way to ascend through the spiky vegetation and rocky outcrops. The summit of **Pico del Tesoro** (1994m; 1hr, 2km) has widespread views in all directions, but in winter the snows of the Sierra Nevada and the nearby Trevenque will catch the eye.

From here, follow the south west ridge of the peak, descending towards the track north of Cerro de la Cortijuela. It is rough going and there is some optional simple rock scrambling which can be avoided on steep loose paths to the left of the ridge. Some superb-looking rock gendarmes guard the lower part before a track is met and a col just east of Cerro de la Cortijuela is reached (1hr 30min, 2.5km).

Alternative route avoiding difficult terrain

The rough descent of Pico del Tesoro via the south west ridge can be avoided entirely by making a return to Collado de Matas Verdes. This alternative keeps to decent tracks throughout and saves 20min.

On the descent and just before reaching **Collado de Matas Verdes**, take a good, well-marked path going off to the right (west); after a further 20min another col just east of Cerro de la Cortijuela is reached and the wide track can be followed in its entirety to rejoin the main route at **Collado Ruquino**.

From the col just east of Cerro de la Cortijuela, easier, broader slopes lead along the ridge and over **Cerro de la Cortijuela** (1859m). There is one section (avoidable on the right) where a short scramble up a gully and along a ridge provides excitement, before the path passes over a broader section of ridge to join the dirt track again at a junction with a good dirt road coming in from the left. This is the col of **Collado Ruquino** (2hr, 4km). Ahead rise the twin peaks of Cerro del Cocón.

Ignore the dirt track and take the path that leads up and along the ridge, running left of the track. It is nicely graded and makes for a more interesting alternative. A short drop north to cross the road (El Collado) is followed by the ascent of the peak. Find the easiest line possible through the arid jumble of stones and boulders; it is 15min of hard work to gain the small but superbly situated summit

The short scrambling section on the Cortijuela ridge (Photo: Ian Tupman)

The dirt road back to Collado Ruquino

of **Cerro del Cocón** (1858m; 2hr 30min, 5km), but it's worth the effort: this is a great place to take a break and enjoy the vistas.

> There are great **views** in all directions. To the east, Pico de Tesoro with Veleta to its right compete with the view across the depths to Trevenque in the south. To the west rise Cerro Gordo and Pico de Carne.

A short 5min drop to the east brings you to the col between the two summits. It's a simple matter to visit the second summit if desired; if not, make the short return to the dirt track at El Collado and follow this easily down to **Collado Ruquino**. Turn right here down the gently descending road to join the Arroyo de Huenes valley road to **Casa Forestal de la Cortijuela**, which is reached in a further 10min.

ROUTE 20
Trevenque direct

Start/Finish	Casa Forestal de la Cortijuela
Distance	5km
Total ascent	330m
Grade	Moderate (due to the rough, steep ascent to the summit)
Time	3hr
Summits	Trevenque
Water sources	Spring at Casa Forestal de la Cortijuela
Seasonal notes	In high summer (due to fire risk) or after fresh winter snowfall, the access road north of Arroyo de Huenes can be closed 1km west of Puente de Siete Ojos. In this case a walk up the valley and a return traversing the mountain may be the best alternative route.

If time is of the essence, this is the shortest and quickest way to ascend Trevenque. It is also the steepest, with some rough ground to ascend (and descend!). Suitable for those who like their mountains rough and tough!

Close to the refuge are the **Botanical Gardens**, which serve to protect, conserve, regenerate and research the flora of the area – especially in the 60+ important endemic species that live there.

It is free to visit and opens Tuesday to Sunday between 10am and 4pm. Due to the altitude, the gardens are closed between November and February. There are 2.5km of well laid-out trails involving a 100m height gain. Vulnerable plants or those in danger of extinction are clearly identified.

The route starts from the Casa, although it is sometimes possible to drive cars past this point and through the forest for nearly 1.8km to a sharp left-hand bend where Trevenque rises ahead and a track branches off to the right. The car can be parked here. If, however, there is a chain across the road at Casa Forestal de la Cortijuela and vehicle access is restricted, it's an easy enough walk.

From the corner of the dirt road take the path leading south for 100m reach **Collado del Trevenque**, then take a track to the right which meanders across the arid northern flanks of some small hills to start the ascent proper. From here the route to the summit looks quite steep and intimidating, but the path is very clear all the way. It is steep and loose but no scrambling is involved, and you should reach the summit of **Trevenque** (2079m) 45min after leaving the forest track. Enjoy the expansive views in all directions – but especially east to the gleaming snows of the Sierra Nevada.

The return journey is made the same way: retrace steps from the summit for a few minutes, and at the junction of paths with the Cuerda del Trevenque descent route make sure to continue down the path you ascended (it's easy to take the wrong path at this point!).

Far below, amid the chaotic waste of arid badlands, lies the col of Collado del Trevenque, where you'll rejoin the forest road. Take care on the steep and loose initial descent slopes; thereafter the descent is marked by short steep sections

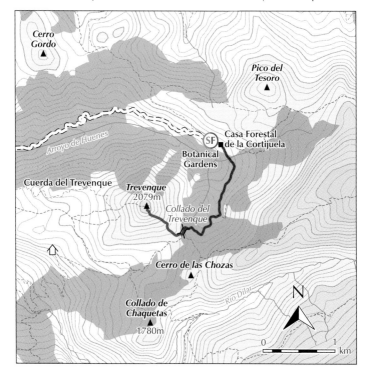

The lower path with arid badlands to the right

intermingled with easier walking. Towards the bottom, bypass some small hills on the left and reach **Collado del Trevenque**. Turn left for 100m and rejoin the forest road, which is followed back to the start.

SKI AREA – HOYA DE LA MORA

Collado de Carihuela with the Tajos de la Virgen ridge behind (Route 22)

The **Sierra Nevada ski town** (also referred to as Pradollano or its old name, Sol y Nieve) is situated between 2000m and 2400m on the northern slopes of Veleta, giving easy and convenient year-round access to the higher peaks.

In the winter months (December to April inclusive) the ski town comes alive, with thousands packing into the rather ugly and garish multi-storey hotels and apartment blocks. Restaurants and bars abound with the après-ski crowds.

By contrast, during the summer months (May to November) the town reverts to its close-season status and becomes almost a ghost town. Few hotels remain open, although there are a few hostels catering for the walking and trekking business – most notably the Albergue Universitario de Granada, situated above the ski town at Hoya de la Mora (2500m). In July and August a ski lift opens to take walkers and mountain bikers to the cooler air of 3000m.

A guarded hostel, Albergue Universitario Sierra Nevada, is situated at 2500m near Peñones de San Francisco and adjacent to Hoya de la Mora. It is open all year, has serviced accommodation, a restaurant, café, and a leisure lounge with a large fireplace. See Appendix B for details.

The old road linking Granada with Veleta was the highest road in Europe. A colossal work of engineering, it was completed and officially opened in 1935. Many years later, in 1966, the section that continues to the Alpujarras was concluded. Today it is closed to traffic on both sides – at Hoya de la Mora (2500m) on the Veleta side and at Hoya del Portillo (2150m) in the Alpujarras.

Getting to the ski area

From the main Granada ring road (Circunvalación), follow the well-signposted mountain road to Sierra Nevada (A-395). This leads to the main ski resort at Pradollano. At km30, just before entering the resort, turn left following signs to Hoya de la Mora and Albergues de Granada. At km35 (2500m altitude) the road ends and there are car parks on either side. This is Hoya de la Mora.

After new snowfall the access road to Hoya de la Mora can become blocked, and it is the last road to be cleared and opened by the ski lift company. Access may be possible with snow chains; in this case you can turn right at km31 and follow the signs to a large car park at Telesilla de las Nieves. This is a little below Hoya de la Mora and necessitates a short uphill walk (30min), following the car park access road north for 100m before turning south onto the main access road.

On weekends and during *fiestas* (public holidays) this area can become heavily congested with families eager to toboggan down the slopes leading to the car parks. The police at times restrict numbers and close the road. An early start is essential.

ROUTE 21

Veleta, Tajos de la Virgen and Lagunillas

Start/Finish	Hoya de la Mora
Distance	17km
Total ascent	850m
Grade	Challenging
Time	7hr 30min
Summits	Veleta, Puntal de Loma Púa, Tajos de la Virgen
Water sources	Lagunillas de la Virgen
Seasonal notes	Winter lasts a long time in this area and snow will normally be found on this route until mid June. Watch out for the large cornice build-up at Posiciones del Veleta. The Tajos de la Virgen ridge is a winter mountaineering route, but watch the descent back from Refugio Elorrieta as this can be avalanche-prone.

A circular day-walk ascending Veleta – at 3394m the second highest peak in the Sierra Nevada – and continuing over the Tajos de la Virgen ridge to Refugio Elorrieta. A return is made via the beautiful lakes at Lagunillas de la Virgen. There are a couple of simple scrambling sections on the ridge (avoidable by an alternative route), but otherwise the route follows good paths throughout.

From Hoya de la Mora, ascend the broad northern slopes of Veleta on a variety of well-marked tracks that pass either side of the **Virgen de las Nieves** statue and left of the Telesilla de la Virgen chairlift station. There are plenty of options, but the best stays away from the ski detritus and old road and keeps the escarpment edge of Barranco de San Juan to the left. The ascent to the 3100m northern shoulder of Veleta, named **Posiciones del Veleta**, should take just less than 2hr.

> **Posiciones del Veleta** is a marvellous viewpoint in its own right. Take a wander out east from the old road to the edge overlooking the spectacular Corral del Veleta. Alcazaba, Mulhacén and Cerro de los Machos are prominent across the Corral.

There are three options for reaching the summit of **Veleta** from here: you can either keep as close to the edge of the ridge as possible as it curves leftwards to the summit (this requires a head for heights and some scrambling ability); or you can stay on the old road as it traverses west of the summit, gaining height gradually and looking out for a path near a ski sign for 'Descenso Hombres' that leads uphill through the scree to the left, then joining the ridge crest higher up to the left and following it to the summit (this makes for a more interesting ascent – although it is just a walk, with no scrambling nor a head for heights required); or thirdly you could continue on the old road until it splits, and then take the left branch which meanders and zig-zags up the gentle south west face of the mountain to easily reach the summit (3hr, 5.5km).

> The relatively gentle western and south western aspects of **Veleta** contrast greatly with the precipices found of the north and east when looking down from the summit cairn. Most of the Sierra Nevada 3000m peaks can be seen from this vantage point. Away to the west, the Vega de Granada plains merge into the coastal mountains around Málaga.

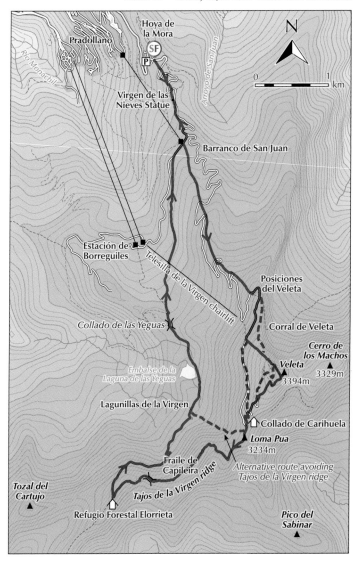

The Tajos de la Virgen ridge seen from Veleta, with Cerro de Caballo in the background

The way to the next objective, the pass of Collado de Carihuela, involves dropping down to the south west, and again the best path for views is the one that keeps as close to the edge of the escarpment as possible. The going is easy, with vistas over the Tajos de la Virgen ridge and beyond to Cerro del Caballo and the sparking Mediterranean Sea. **Collado de Carihuela**, with the tiny Refugio Vivac de la Carihuela lying just to the east, is reached in under 30min from the summit of Veleta.

> In early morning or late evening, and especially in winter, it is not uncommon to be able to see the line of the **Rif mountains** of Morocco on the horizon.

From the col you have two options: you can either continue on the main route along the Tajos de la Virgen ridge, which involves some scrambling, or you can avoid the ridge altogether and descent directly to Lagunillas de la Virgen.

Alternative descent avoiding scrambling
This option avoids all scrambling and saves 1hr 45min, 150m ascent and 4km.
Descend directly west on a path – well marked but steep in places – through the scree west of Colllado de Carihuela and down the 'Olympica' winter ski run. After 250m (40min) of descent, arrive at the beautiful area of small lakes known as **Lagunillas de la Virgen** – a fine place to take a break. Rejoin the main route here.

Start the Tajos de la Virgen ridge proper by climbing **Puntal de Loma Pua** (3234m). Many parties bypass this on the right-hand side and gain the ridge beyond. From here there is a delightful ridge crest interspersed with easy rocky sections. After 30min a rock tower (3228m) blocks the way; climb easily up the tower until you're 20m below the top and then traverse the slanting ledges in an exposed situation on the right-hand side.

Easier going follows on a broader ridge: pass left of the rocky 20m-high gendarme known as the **Fraile de Capileira** and make a descending traverse to a **col** before another rock step (3191m) bars the way. Take a traverse line left for 50m before climbing right back up a narrow rake to the ridge line, above the step. From here the ruined **Refugio Elorrieta** (3160m; 5hr, 9.5km) is easily reached via a blocky ridge.

Descend first north and then north east from the refuge. After 10min, cross a steep convex slope which traverses below Tajos de la Virgen, and descend gradually to the lakes of **Lagunillas de la Virgen** (6hr, 11.5km)

Leave the lakes and follow the very well-marked path northwards past the eastern shore of **Embalse de las Yeguas** to reach a dirt track. This leads easily over the col of **Collado de Las Yeguas** (6hr 30min, 13km), down into the ski area and towards **Estación de Borreguiles**. From here it's an easy 45min walk back to **Hoya de la Mora**.

Lagunillas de la Virgen in the spring. A relaxing place to while away the hours!

ROUTE 22

Veredón Superior and Cerro de los Machos

Start/Finish	Hoya de la Mora
Distance	12.5km
Total ascent	870m
Grade	Challenging
Time	6hr 15min
Summits	Cerro de los Machos
Water sources	In the Corral del Veleta and the south eastern slopes of Veleta below Collado de Carihuela
Seasonal notes	This whole route becomes much more serious under winter conditions, when it is necessary to abseil into the Corral in order to avoid the cornices.

A superbly varied circular walk visiting the dramatic bowl of the Corral del Veleta and ascending the lesser-known peak of Cerro de los Machos (3329m). Optional interest and excitement can be added to the return journey by crossing Paso de las Guías en route to Collado de Carihuela.

A summer bus service from Albergue de Granada at Hoya de la Mora goes to Posiciones del Veleta, shortening the initial outward walk by nearly 4km and 570m ascent. From Hoya de la Mora, ascend the broad northern slopes of Veleta on a variety of well-marked tracks that pass either side of the **Virgen de las Nieves** statue and left of the Telesilla de la Virgen chairlift station. There are plenty of options, but the best stays away from the ski detritus and old road and keeps the escarpment edge of Barranco de San Juan to the left. The ascent to the 3100m northern shoulder of Veleta, named **Posiciones del Veleta**, should take just less than 2hr.

> **Posiciones del Veleta** is a marvellous viewpoint in its own right. Take a wander out east from the old road to the edge overlooking the spectacular Corral del Veleta. Alcazaba, Mulhacén and Cerro de los Machos are prominent across the Corral.

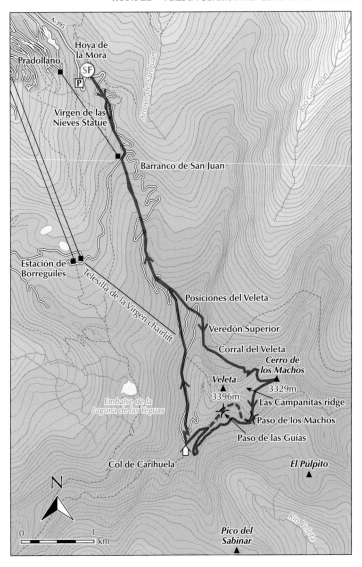

Walk 250m up the road towards Veleta and take the path (**Veredón Superior**) that leaves the road and trends left into the upper valley of the Corral del Veleta. At a small col the whole of the Corral opens out – a spectacular scene.

THE CORRAL DEL VELETA ROCK GLACIER

The Corral del Veleta is what's called a 'rock glacier' – an accumulation of snow and ice of low volume that does not have the ability to move and is covered by material erosion. Thus the ice is not visible. These are also known as 'black glaciers'.

Today, the ice of this geomorphological structure is only 10 metres thick. The normal trend is that this mass of ice beneath the rocks loses between 50cm and 70cm each year. This degradation is part of the natural process of any glacier, although with warmer temperatures the process could be accelerated.

A group of researchers from the University of Extremadura have shown that the rock glacier in the Corral del Veleta could disappear in the coming 20 years. Their calculations are based on normal temperatures, but if these increase then the degradation process will be accelerated.

The Corral del Veleta was the last place in the Sierra Nevada to be glaciated, and the valley floor itself shows signs of the moraines. Behind these, some small lakes can be found. Indeed, snow can remain in some isolated sheltered places throughout the year, especially after heavy winter snowfalls.

Drop steeply on the path into the **Corral**. Dropping into the Corral the sheer scale of the place is felt for the first time with huge rock walls towering above. There is the initial feeling that it will be a little exposed, but the reality is that this is a good path and the exposure is hardly felt at all on descent.

Alternative start from Posiciones del Veleta

In high summer an alternative start would be to use the ski lifts or bus to access Posiciones del Veleta. Use the Veredón Superior to drop into the Corral de Veleta and hence down into the Guarnón valley to join the main route prior to the ascent to the Collado de Veta Grande.

Cross the valley floor and climb the scree slope of **Cerro de los Machos** opposite. A path hugs the lip of the retaining moraine, and at the far end of the valley a series of steep zig-zags rise through the scree. It is arduous but leads rapidly to the easier ground above the Corral. There is a superb moment when the view opens

THE TÚNEL DEL VELETA

There is a tunnel situated on an east-facing wall just left of the path at the lip of the Corral which dates back to the time of the old road construction in the 1930s. The initial plan was that the road, instead of skirting Veleta by Collado de Carihuela, would go through a tunnel starting from near Posiciones and leading into the Corral del Veleta. The road would then continue over Cerro de los Machos and hence to the Alpujarras in the south.

But it didn't happen. Both sides of the tunnel never got to meet. Some 170m of tunnel about 30m wide was dug out from the Corral del Veleta side before work was abandoned. The old tunnel is now used as a makeshift and often welcome shelter for mountaineers.

out to the south. Turn left and walk the final few metres to the fine summit cairn of **Cerro de los Machos** (3329m; 3hr 30min, 5.5km).

It's an isolated **summit**. To the north is the narrow ridge leading down to Veta Grande (2983m), and to the west is the ridge of Las Campanitas leading to Veleta itself (see Route 37). Both routes are best left to expert scramblers.

View east to Alcazaba and Mulhacén from the summit of Cerro de los Machos

The short, spectacular but straightforward Paso de las Guías (Photo: Felipe Nieto Conejero)

The only safe and straightforward way off is to follow the broad ridge south west. Find the path just left of the first pinnacle on the Las Campanitas ridge; this leads easily down to the old road just west of **Paso de Los Machos**, 30min from the summit (4hr, 6.5km).

There are now two options to get to the col of Collado de Carihuela: you can either follow the old road (easy, 30min) or use Paso de Las Guías (20min). The latter is shorter but involves some exposure as the route crosses a short 30m section of vertical wall assisted by a chain.

Paso de Las Guías alternative
This option only saves 10min over the main route but it adds interest.

A few metres from the junction of the path descending from Cerro de los Machos and the old road, veer right on a path that leads round the south western bowl of Veleta to arrive very quickly at a short section of chain-assisted track. Once through it is only 10min to rejoin the old road and reach the refuge and **Collado de Carihuela**.

From Collado de Carihuela follow the ski road as it slowly descends back to **Posiciones** and hence to **Hoya de la Mora**.

ROUTE 23

Veredón Inferior, Veta Grande, northern flanks and lakes

Start/Finish	Hoya de la Mora
Alternative start	Posiciones del Veleta
Distance	21km
Total ascent	1440m
Grade	Tough
Time	11hr/2 days
Summits	Juego de Bolos, Veta Grande
Water sources	There is abundant water on this route throughout even the driest of summers
Seasonal notes	Under snow and ice conditions this is for winter mountaineers only. By late June the trail is normally open for trekkers until the snows arrive again in late autumn.

This is a tough and remote trek, doable in one long hard day or preferably by taking advantage of some superlative campsite locations and splitting it into two days. It covers quiet, rarely frequented and spectacular paths along the northern flanks and valleys of the central Sierra Nevada, followed by an easy return along the old road. There is some exposure descending the Veredón Inferior, but no scrambling involved on the route described.

Potential camping spots can be found at Lagunillo de la Galbata, Laguna Larga, Laguna de la Caldera and Lagunas de Río Seco.

From Hoya de la Mora take the well-worn path that leads up and passes right of the old **observatory** on Mojón del Trigo, then traverse on a path down into **Barranco de San Juan**. Cross the river and climb directly east over pathless terrain to the ridge of **Tajos del Campanario**.

The ridge gives a pleasant walk with the cliffs to the east providing constant interest. Just below the 3000m level there is a prominent step in the ridge with a metal cross attached; this marks your entry, left, into the spectacular path known as the **Veredón Inferior** (2hr, 4km), which descends to the valley of the Río Guarnón. The path is narrow and rock looms both above and below as it traverses

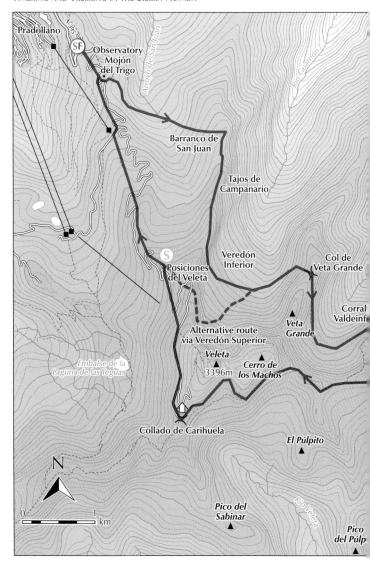

the cliff face before dropping down to the valley. Some exposure is felt but it is just a walk – no scrambling involved.

There is no obvious path across the valley floor but the zig-zag path on the other side, which climbs up through the screes to the col before Veta Grande, is obvious and it is the base of this you should aim for.

The **valley of the Río Guarnón** is awash with streams and green pastures, or *borreguiles*. It is full of life in early summer and a wonderful place to rest before the somewhat gruelling ascent to the col on Veta Grande.

It's a tough, steep slog through the screes of the western slopes of Veta Grande; however, it is soon over and forgotten as you reach **Col de Veta Grande** (2950m; 3hr 45min, 6km), where a marvellous view opens out to the east. From the col the peak of Veta Grande is 0.5km (140m ascent) to the south.

This is possibly one of the best **views** in the whole range. The dramatic northern flanks of the central massif are rarely seen from these angles and are much more spectacular than those in the south. Dotted in the valleys are numerous tiny lakes, with streams tumbling down the steep hillsides and cliffs originating from Crestones de Río Seco, Puntal de Laguna Larga and the Puntal de la Caldera mountains. As a backdrop you also have the northern faces of both Mulhacén and Alcazaba.

Alcazaba and Mulhacén from Col de Veta Grande

Take a faint path that traverses and drops steadily into the head of **Corral de Valdeinfierno** – almost as wild a place as you can possibly get. Pass some small lakes and streams and continue round the valley head to cross a shoulder that leads down to the superbly situated lakes of Lagunillo de la Galbata and **Laguna Larga** (5hr, 8.5km).

Laguna Larga nestles beneath the huge north west face of Puntal de la Caldera

> For those on a two-day trek, these **lakes** are without a shadow of a doubt the place to stay. The steep, loose cliffs of Puntal de Laguna Larga rise above, contrasting with the greenery and lushness of the lakeside. Below the lakes, streams tumble down into the Valdeinfierno valley. A magical place!

Follow the path as it heads north of Laguna Larga and rises slightly before continuing round the shoulder of **Espolón de la Caldera** (see scrambling Route 36) It crosses a gully before ascending some steep scree to the strangely named peak of **Juego de Bolos** ('game of balls', 3019m; 6hr 30min, 10km). Juego de Bolos forms the western arm of the valley containing Laguna de la Mosca.

From the peak the best route is to follow the ridge line south as much as possible (some simple scrambling is avoidable to the right of the ridge) until faint tracks lead leftwards, traversing towards the col of **Collado del Ciervo** (7hr 30min, 11km).

From here it's a simple matter to drop down to **Refugio Vivac de la Caldera** and follow the wide trail over the col between Loma Pelada and Puntal de Laguna Larga to join the old road at **Crestones de Río Seco**, continuing onwards to **Collado de Carihuela** (9hr 15min, 16km). From the col, follow the old road. Before reaching Posiciones del Veleta turn left down a well-trodden path which heads easily down and back to **Hoya de la Mora**. There are plenty of well-trodden paths passing through or on the edge of the ski pistes, leading northwards back to the start point.

ROUTE 24

Across the mountains to Lanjarón via Refugio Elorrieta

Start	Hoya de la Mora
Finish	Lanjarón
Distance	29km
Total ascent	860m
Total descent	2720m
Grade	Tough
Time	11hr/2 days
Summits	Tozal de Cartujo, Tajos Altos, Cerro de Caballo
Water sources	Lagunillas de la Virgen, Río Lanjarón valley. None on main ridge to Cerro del Caballo.
Seasonal notes	A major undertaking in winter, best done on skis. The slopes below the Tajos de la Virgen ridge are prone to avalanche but the Valle de Lanjarón makes a superb descent.

There are many ways to cross the Sierra Nevada in long day-trips or on multi-day trips, and most involve using the old road at some point. This route avoids the road and links the ski area in the north with the town of Lanjarón in the south.

Best done north to south to take advantage of the high start-point at Hoya de la Mora, the route can be done in one long summer day. However, it is much preferable to take advantage of some delectable camping locations and make it a two-day trek. There are lots of opportunities for variations and side-trips along the way.

Potential camping spots can be found at Laguna de Lanjarón, Charca Pala, Laguna de Bolaños, Laguna Cuadrada and Laguna de Caballo. There are some nice options alongside the river in the upper Lanjarón valley. On the main ridge line a col just 500m south west of Tajos Altos has level ground and a cave (but no water in the summer).

From Hoya de la Mora, initially follow the paths towards Veleta up to the first **chair lift station** on the right (Telesilla Virgen de las Nieves), then keep right and continue on the road above the station. Some 200m further on, at a snow fence, take the path that leaves the road and trends off to the left. (The road can be followed in its entirety to Borreguiles but the path offers a more pleasant experience.)

The path continues above the ski station buildings at **Borreguiles** and easily up to the pass of **Collado de las Yeguas**. Follow the track as it leads past the large reservoir of **Embalse de las Yeguas** itself and onto the small lakes at **Lagunillas** (1hr 45min, 5.5km). From here make a rising traverse on a good path below and north west of the Tajos de la Virgen ridge to **Refugio Elorrieta** (3hr, 7km).

REFUGIO ELORRIETA

There is a spectacular view from the refuge, both back to the main peaks of the Sierra Nevada and also south west towards the ridge line of peaks leading to Cerro del Caballo. The refuge has fallen into disrepair and is unfortunately in a sorry state; despite this, it is an interesting place to have a look around – in particular at an old series of tunnels. It also makes one of the finest places in the Sierra Nevada to see the sunset and sunrise in all their glory.

The curious square of cleared ground on the col below the refuge was an attempt many years ago by reforestation workers to see if cultivation at these altitudes was possible. Evidently not!

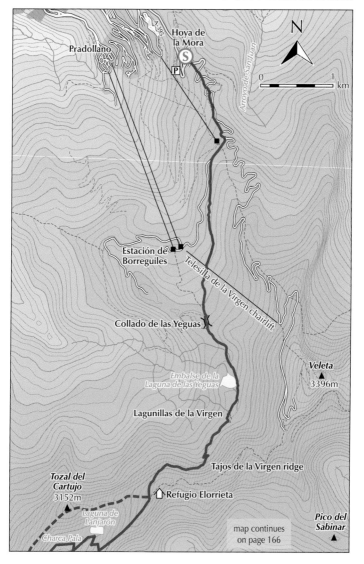

Pradollano

Hoya de
la Mora

S

P

N

Arroyo de San Juan

0   1
km

Estación de
Borreguiles

Telesilla de la Virgen chairlift

Collado de las Yeguas

Veleta
3396m

Embalse de la
Laguna de las Yeguas

Lagunillas de la Virgen

Tajos de la Virgen ridge

Tozal del
Cartujo
3152m

Refugio Elorrieta

Laguna de
Lanjarón

Charca Pala

Pico del
Sabinar

map continues
on page 166

165

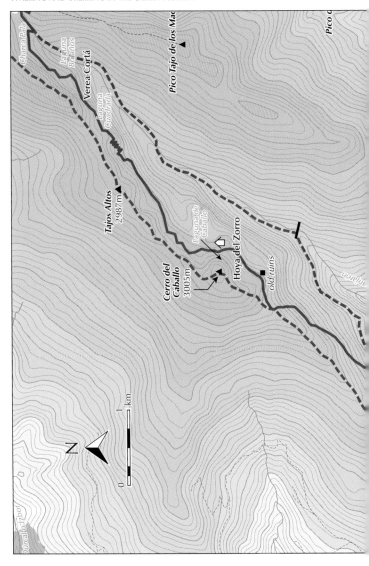

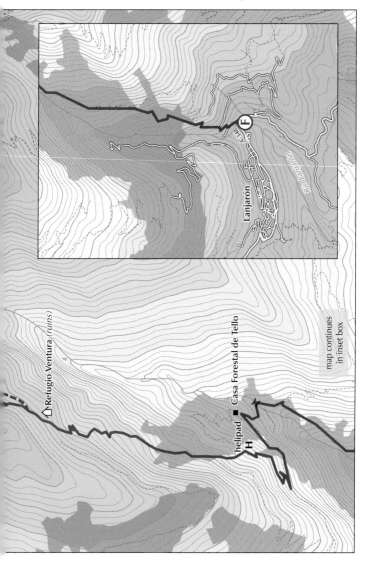

Lanjarón

Río Lanjarón

Refugio Ventura (ruins)

Casa Forestal de Tello

helipad

map continues in inset box

There are three options for reaching Refugio Ventura from Refugio Elorrieta; the Verea Cortá route is the most interesting and entertaining and is described here as the 'main' route.

Follow the path south west from the refuge – it maintains height before dropping towards **Laguna de Lanjarón** (3hr 45min, 8km).

The Laguna de Lanjarón is a 'shangri-la' or sacred place for the people of Lanjarón to visit. It is the reason for the town's very existence: the Río Lanjarón flows out of the lake, supplying life-bearing waters from the high Sierras.

The mid-level path starts just below the lake and traverses the mountainside, visiting the beautifully situated lakes of **Charca Pala**, **Laguna de Bolaños** and **Laguna Cuadrada** to arrive at the lake and **refuge** below Cerro del Caballo (5hr 30min, 13km). There is a short section of chain to assist progress across a steep gully just a few hundred metres north east of Laguna Cuadrada – the **Verea Cortá** – but this is nothing to worry about. A few steps holding the chain and you're across. The exposure is not great.

From the Refugio de Caballo follow the path that passes east of the peak, round the entrance to the Hoya del Zorro valley to some **old ruins** south of the peak. From here descend on a scree path east of the ridge line and **Morra Alta** to join the *acequia* (irrigation channel) path just above the semi-ruined **Refugio Ventura** (7hr, 18km).

Routes from the Refugio Elorrieta to the Cerro de Caballo

Laguna Cuadrada from the ridge south east of Tozal de Cartujo, with Cerro de Caballo in the distance

Alternative route from Elorrieta to Ventura via Lanjarón valley

The upper Lanjarón valley provides the easiest route, saving an hour, 200m of ascent and 1km over the main route.

Follow the path south west from Refugio Elorrieta – it maintains height before dropping to **Laguna de Lanjarón**. From here, follow the *río* (river) on paths that alternate between the left and right banks.

> The **upper Lanjarón valley** is a fascinating place to be – especially in late spring when tunnels of snow form over the fast-flowing river. The sound of bells signifies the return of cattle, sheep and goats from their lower winter pastures and the whole valley seems alive and vibrant.

Pass below **Cerro del Caballo** to reach a **small dam** across the river at the entrance to the valley – this provides an infallible guide for the next section. Pass right (west) of the dam and descend on the path to join an *acequia* (irrigation channel) which is very easily followed until just above Refugio Ventura. Here a post signifies a path going downhill to the left; take this to reach the **refuge** (3hr from Refugio Elorrieta).

Alternative route from Elorrieta to Ventura via the high ridge

This route forms part of 'Los Tres Miles Integral' – see Route 31. This option adds one hour, 200m of ascent and 1km to the main route.

The initial way west from Refugio Elorrieta in untracked but crosses a stony plateau en route to the ridge opposite. The path is faint in places, but small cairns indicate the route. At one point on the ridge crest there is an awkward step down, followed immediately at a cairn by a short downward traverse on the western (right) side of the ridge. In front a large cliff bars the way but is easily avoided by a path to the left, which then ascends without difficulty to **Tozal del Cartujo** (3152m).

The way south west is obvious, although tracks are sometimes faint. Don't be tempted to avoid the summit of **Tajos Altos** (2987m) by a flanking path as it's a fine summit in its own right. Cerro del Caballo lies some 2km away from here over an undulating ridge.

Continue over the summit of **Cerro del Caballo** (3005m) and round the bowl south of the peak to join the main route at the ruins just after Hoya del Zorro (4hr from Refugio Elorrieta). To get to Refugio Ventura the best advice in good weather is to stick to the long south ridge until nearly above the **refuge**, where a direct pathless descent can be made to the *acequia* (irrigation channel) above it (5hr from Refugio Elorrieta).

The sparkling waters of the Río Lanjarón provide an easier route southwards – especially rewarding in late spring

The track below the Refugio Ventura with the Cerro de Caballo rising behind. The upper Lanjarón valley exits from the right

Main route from the refuge

At Refugio Ventura (2250m) you might be forgiven for thinking that the bulk of the journey has been completed; but there is still some 1600m of unremitting descent ahead.

Take the path leading past the refuge and within 15min arrive at a dirt road. Your next objective is Casa Forestal de Tello – some white-painted buildings set next to the Río Lanjarón at 1700m. The route down to these ruins changed dramatically after a major wildfire in September 2005, and in 2017 maps still didn't reflect the route accurately. However, the 'new' route is quite obvious – although there are a variety of options. The infallible advice in any difficulties is to follow the dirt road until above an obvious **helipad** situated alongside another dirt road. Paths drop down to this and the dirt track can be followed initially north east before returning south east to **Casa Forestal de Tello** (8hr 45min, 24km).

Below Tello take the path that crosses the **Río Lanjarón**, from where a well-signposted drovers' path (Camino de las Sierras) follows the eastern bank of the river to the town of **Lanjarón**. There are regular buses from Lanjarón to Granada and onwards to Guadix/Jerez de Marquesado (**www.alsa.es/en**).

VEREDA DE LA ESTRELLA/GENIL VALLEY

Alcazaba and Mulhacén north faces from the path leading to Cortijos del Hornillo (Photo: Victoria Bocanegra Montañes) (Route 26)

There is no doubt that the most dramatic and spectacular views of the Sierra Nevada are from the north. The north faces of Mulhacén and Alcazaba fall precipitously into deep and savage valleys; a total contrast to the more genteel nature of the southern slopes. The Genil valley gives access to this side of the range, using the Vereda de Estrella trail for both day-walks and multi-day trekking adventures.

Closest to the trailhead is the pleasant and traditional town of **Güéjar Sierra** with a population of around 3000. It has some small hotels – notably the Hotel Rural Mirasierra – and plenty of guest houses, hostels and apartments for rent. There is no shortage of restaurants and bars either. Some may prefer the big city life in **Granada** and make the short journey to the trailhead from there.

Getting to Vereda de la Estrella
(6.5km, 15min from Güéjar Sierra)
Vereda de la Estrella is the start-point for Routes 25, 26, 27 and 28.

The town of Güéjar Sierra (1000m) is very easily reached from Granada city in 30min via the A-395 (Cenes de la Vega and Pinos Genil), while access to the Sierra Nevada from Güéjar Sierra usually involves a lot of hard work as the

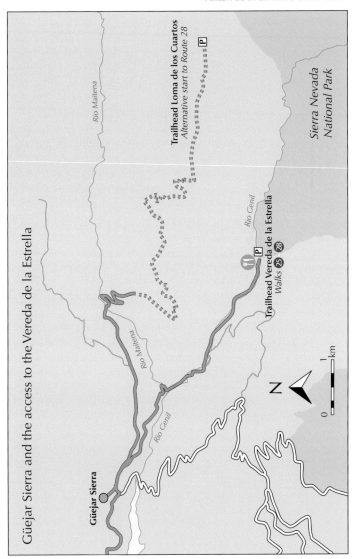

Güéjar Sierra and the access to the Vereda de la Estrella

Trailhead Loma de los Cuartos
Alternative start to Route 28

Río Maitena

Sierra Nevada
National Park

Río Genil

Trailhead Vereda de la Estrella
Walks 25 28

Río Maitena

Río Genil

Güéjar Sierra

N

0 — 1 km

distances are long and the start-points are low. Take the main road east of Güéjar Sierra, well-signposted to the start of the Vereda de la Estrella. This narrow road drops steadily down to the Río Genil and passes through a series of tunnels on its way to the trailhead, where there is a restaurant and car park.

Getting to Loma de los Cuartos
(14km, 40min from Güéjar Sierra)
Loma de los Cuartos is an alternative start-point for Route 28.

This is a well-used road from Güéjar Sierra that crosses the Río Maitena and ascends Loma de los Cuartos, a long west-east ridge. Just after leaving Güéjar Sierra turn left and follow a narrow road for 2km. Just after passing through an obvious rock cutting turn right. The road drops down to cross the Río Maítena. Shortly after this it turns into a dirt track. At junctions follow signs for Lavaderos de la Reina or take the track showing the most signs of use. The ridge of Loma de los Cuartos is met at a fire lookout point and superb views to the north faces of the Sierra Nevada open out. Follow the dirt track until a chain across the road indicates where cars must be left. It's only a 2hr gentle walk east over Papeles (2424m) to Refugio Peña Partida from here. The lower half of the road is in very good condition but the upper section very rough; a 4WD vehicle is recommended, although saloon cars of all shapes and sizes frequently use the track.

ROUTE 25
Vereda de la Estrella, Refugio Cucaracha and Cueva Secreta

Start/Finish	Trailhead, Vereda de la Estrella
Distance	21km
Total ascent	1250m
Grade	Challenging
Time	8hr
Water sources	Plentiful in the Río Genil
Seasonal notes	In winter the Vereda de la Estrella path alongside the Río Genil can be very icy – especially where sub-streams cross the path. There have been accidents here and crampons are sometimes necessary. Probably too hot in July and August for comfortable walking.

The Vereda de la Estrella walk should not be missed. A circular route around the Río Genil with some classic views of the north faces of Alcazaba (3371m) and Mulhacén (3482m), the walking is on generally good paths with extensive views of the surrounding mountains opening up as the hike progress. There are some short steep ascents and descents, however, with some rough sections.

Leave the car park, cross the bridge and turn left onto the 'Vereda de la Estrella' path. Follow this for 3km to a signpost and junction of paths. (After 1km the Sulayr GR240 path joins in from the right – its marker posts will show the way until Refugio Forestal La Cucaracha is reached.)

The going is easy along this southern side of the valley, passing wooded sections of **chestnut trees**, which are abundant in this area (including one of 100 years old called 'The Grandfather').

Bridge over the Río Guarnón (Photo: Victoria Bocanegra Montañes)

At the junction of paths, turn left down the hill to cross the Río Genil near the ruined **Refugio Vadillo** at Puente de los Burros. The steepest and most arduous part of the day now follows as the track climbs 3km up the Cuesta de los Presidiarios to reach **Refugio Forestal La Cucaracha** at 1750m (2hr 30min, 6.5km). Always to the south are dramatic vistas of the north faces of Mulhacén and Alcazaba.

The Sulayr path is now left behind. Cross the fence and continue past the refuge. The undulating path heads south for a further 2km – with spectacular views ahead – until the dramatically placed **Refugio Aceral** is reached (3hr 30min, 8km).

175

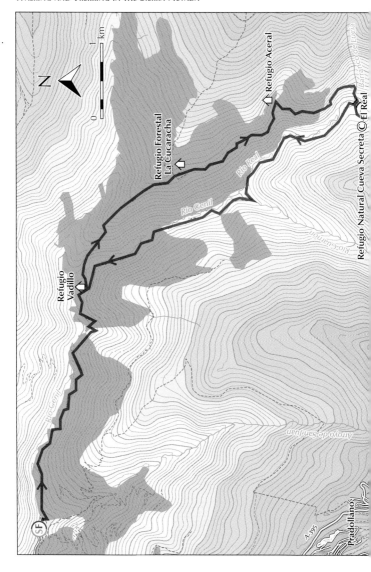

Just past the refuge, cross the *barranco* (gorge) of Barranco del Aceral (water may be available here) and then follow the path down to the right for 1.5km until a right fork at **Barranco de Lucia** allows descent to the river and bridge at **El Real**. Cross the bridge and rejoin the Vereda de Estrella path.

It is worth a slight detour south here to visit the natural shelters at **Refugio Natural Cueva Secreta**. This is a natural refuge and is a popular and convenient place to bivouac on excursions into the higher Sierra Nevada from the north. It can be reached in 10min by keeping to the path on the western side of the Río Valdeinfiernos. Return the same way.

Continue down the Vereda de la Estrella path as it accompanies the Río Genil. About 2km after leaving the cueva, the **Río Guarnón** valley comes in from the left and the river is crossed by a bridge. The return is long but obvious as yellow-and-white markerposts show the way, and interest is maintained by the beautiful valley, river, waterfalls and ancient mine workings that give the path its name.

ROUTE 26
Cortijos del Hornillo circular

Start/Finish	Trailhead, Vereda de la Estrella
Distance	13.5km
Total ascent	750m
Grade	Moderate
Time	5hr
Water sources	Only alongside the Río Genil
Seasonal notes	In winter the Vereda de la Estrella path alongside the Río Genil can be very icy – especially where sub-streams cross the path. There have been accidents here and crampons are sometimes necessary. Probably too hot in July and August for comfortable walking.

A short but interesting circular walk on the southern side of the Río Genil to visit the Cortijos del Hornillo and their spectacular views south to the major peaks of the Sierra Nevada.

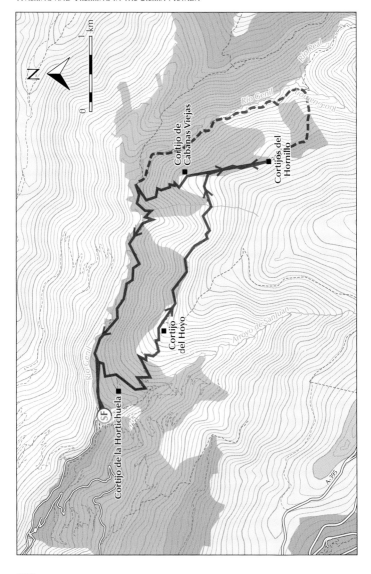

Near Cortijo del Hoyo, with a view up to Penones de San Fransisco near Hoya de la Mora (Photo: Victoria Bocanegra Montañes)

From the trailhead, cross the bridge and take the path opposite going left up the Vereda de Estrella, signposted 'Vrda de la Estrella, Vadillo, C. Secreta'. Follow this for 1km until a path comes in from the right (the Sulayr GR240, marked by red-and-white posts); take this and climb the hillside towards **Cortijo de la Hortichuela**. Note that the Penebetica map shows the wrong access path to Cortijo de la Hortichuela. Continue on the dirt road, always keeping to the higher road until a path on the right near an animal enclosure indicates the way forward.

The main effort on this hike now begins as the path zig-zags up to **Cortijo del Hoyo** at nearly 1800m (1hr 30min, 3.5km). Keep left on the main path; from here the next 2km is much easier as the path contours the mountainside high above the surrounding valleys.

Gradually views open up to the south and the magnificent high mountains of the Sierra Nevada can be seen. About 4km into the walk, just as the path starts to veer to the south, a building is seen on open ground some 200m distant below and to the north. This is the Cortijo de Cabañas Viejas; make a note of this for the return journey. Keeping to the right, the old **Cortijos del Hornillo** are reached a little further on (3hr, 7km).

The **old Cortijos** make a splendid spot to take lunch, with amazing views all around but especially away to the south to Alcazaba and Mulhacén. To the east, across the deep defile of the Río Genil, lie the northern Sierra Nevada peaks from Puntal de los Cuartos to Puntal de Vacares.

Cortijos del Hornillo is one of the few high mountain summer farms still in regular use.

Optional extension

This extension adds 3km (1hr) and provides superb vistas to the south east.

Continue south past Cortijos del Hornillo; the path curves left and drops steeply alongside a stream in a shallow valley to reach the main Vereda de la Estrella path near Cortijos de la Pobadora. Turn left and follow the Vereda de Estrella to the finish. The return is long but obvious as yellow-and-white markerposts show the way, and interest is maintained by the beautiful valley, river, waterfalls and ancient mine workings that give the path its name.

Retrace your steps to just above Cortijo de Cabanas Viejas and follow the path steeply down to the main Vereda de la Estrella path in the valley bottom. Turn left and follow it alongside the Río Genil back to the car park, which is reached in a further 45min.

ROUTE 27
Ascent of Mulhacén via Cueva Secreta

Start	Trailhead, Vereda de la Estrella
Finish	Mulhacén summit
Distance	16km
Total ascent	2790m
Grade	Very tough
Time	9hr
Summits	Mulhacén
Water sources	Plenty of options up to Laguna de la Mosca; limited from there onwards
Seasonal notes	In winter this is a major mountaineering trip, not for winter hill walkers. There are very steep and iced-up slopes below Laguna de la Mosca and often large cornices at Collado del Ciervo. In July and August an early start would avoid the worst of the intense heat on the lower parts of the path.

This is a long trek with a substantial amount of ascent and effort involved to reach the summit of mainland Spain's highest mountain. However, the rewards are also great. There are beautiful rivers, gorges, and without a doubt the most dramatic views of these high mountains. There will be few others too, as many forsake the effort and use the national park bus to reach 2700m from the south. This trek is well worth it for those who like their terrain rough, tough, wild and quiet.

Camping sites can be found at Refugio Forestal Cueva Secreta and Laguna de la Mosca, should you choose to break this walk up with an overnight stay.

Leave the car park and cross the bridge. Turn left onto the 'Vereda de la Estrella' path, which is followed for 3km to a signpost and junction of paths. Follow the path south east alongside the river to **Refugio Natural Cueva Secreta** (3hr, 10.5km).

Cross the Río Valdeinfiernos and trend uphill to join the path alongside the **Río Valdecassillas**. The way ahead looks quite intimidating from here; the ground is steep and the north face of Mulhacén looms above the lip of the bowl

Mulhacén from the north via Collado de Siete Lagunas

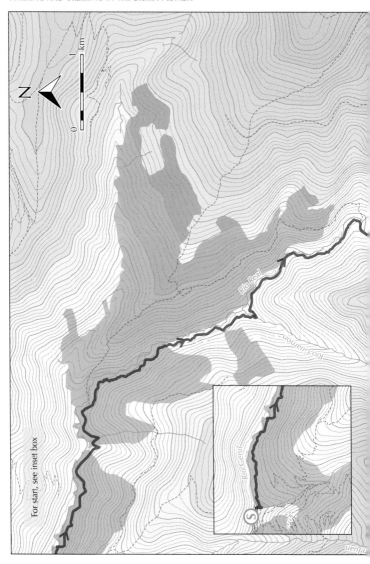

For start, see inset box

Río Real

Río Guarnon

Genil

Río Genil

S

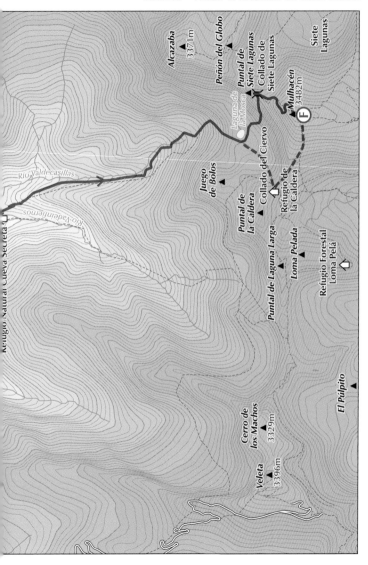

Laguna de la Mosca makes a convenient and beautiful place to break up this ascent

containing Laguna de la Mosca, with Alcazaba to the left and the peak of Juego de Bolos to the right.

Continuing alongside the Río Valdecassillas, the ground steepens considerably until at around 2600m the path swings to the right to cut through the rocks and emerge on the western side of the bowl containing **Laguna de la Mosca**, 4hr from Cueva Secreta.

> **Laguna de la Mosca** is arguably one of the best places to bivouac in the whole of the Sierra Nevada. At dusk it is a serene and atmospheric place to watch the changing light on the cliffs of Alcazaba. Endemic plants and insects thrive in this unique environment. Note though, that the ecosystems here are very fragile, so it is important to bivouac well away from the very inviting grasses (*borreguiles*) next to the lake, and it is illegal to construct stone walls around your tent. The best option is to take to the slightly higher and rockier pre-constructed sites west of the lake.

There are two options to reach the summit from here: our 'main' route goes up to the pass of **Collado de Siete Lagunas** and then via scree gullies and broken ground on the north east to the summit. This is a tough undertaking on steep, loose scree and faint tracks; there are points of mild exposure and some simple scrambling required. Alternatively, a much easier ascent can be made via the west flank.

Easier alternative

The easier option (2hr, 600m ascent) takes the path heading south west from the lake. This becomes more defined as height is gained, and the final steep zig-zags are clearly marked to the col, **Collado del Ciervo**, between Puntal de la Caldera and Mulhacén. From there turn left and climb the west flank to the summit of **Mulhacén** (2.5km from Laguna de la Mosca).

From the lake, the first task is to locate El Corredor de Siete Lagunas. This is a scree gully going up through the crags to the left to reach the pass. Go up the scree cone ahead; there are three left-trending scree gullies – the correct one is in the centre. Ascend this, which links a series of scree slopes. Although loose, there is a path and it is easier than might at first be thought. The path from Vasar de Mulhacén joins in from the right just below the pass.

> The **pass** is a marvellous place to take a break, surrounded by magnificent mountain scenery reminiscent of the Cuillin of Skye. Dramatic views extend in all directions and few others venture here.

The broken north eastern face of Mulhacén now looms above. It doesn't look particularly inviting. The main ridge south from the col takes the form of a series of

The col and Puntal de Siete Lagunas give access to the north east face of Mulhacén. El Corredor de Siete Lagunas is the second gully from the right

shattered buttresses and slabs; it is very broken and loose, so the better option for walkers is to ascend the obvious scree gully slightly to the left.

Ascend the broad gully, which is very loose and will try the patience in summer. At half-height the angle eases beneath a rock face and a move right can be made to a platform overlooking the north face. Go left below the cliff directly above the platform and ascend the scree gully, which is followed by broken ground leading to the summit of **Mulhacén** – or take the alternative option described below.

Alternative route from the platform

A faint path leads right onto the upper part of the north face. Although spectacular, there is surprisingly very little sense of exposure. Continue to traverse rightwards, gaining height to reach another platform. Here a faint path leads back left to regain the north ridge below the summit. Follow the big blocky steps just east of the ridge line until the **Mulhacén** is reached.

OVERNIGHT AND DESCENT OPTIONS

Camps and refuges

It is possible to bivouac on the summit, which is a fine place to watch the spectacular sunsets and sunrises in summer. There are shelters (ruins) just east of the summit that can provide some wind protection. Other overnight options include Refugio de la Caldera (3100m, foot of Mulhacén's west flank), Refugio Forestal Loma Pela (Villavientos) (3090m, south ridge of Loma Pelada) or the guarded Refugio Poqueira (2500m, Río Mulhacén). There are also good camping options at Siete Lagunas (2900m, via Mulhacén's east ridge).

Descent routes from Mulhacén

1   Return to the Vereda de Estrella trailhead: descend Mulhacén's west flank to Collado del Ciervo and from there continue down to Laguna de la Mosca. Here the route of ascent is joined and reversed (8hr).

2   To Trevélez via Siete Lagunas: head south from the summit for 250m to pick up the broad east ridge leading down to Siete Lagunas. Take the well-trodden path without difficulty (besides the amount of metres of descent involved) to the village (4hr 30min).

3   To Trevélez via Alto de Chorrillo: head south on a well-marked and well-cairned path to the south summit, Mulhacén II, then more steeply down to join the old road at a junction with a dirt track leading from

Refugio Poqueira. Follow the road for 200m; it passes east of Alto de Chorrillo (2721m). At a sign, leave the road and follow the path east to the rocks overlooking Trevélez (Mirador de Trevélez). The path drops down the steep hillside in a series of zig-zags; the route is clearly marked and eventually emerges at the highest point of the north west corner of the village (Barrio Alto) (4hr).

4   To Capileira via Barranco del Poqueira: descend Mulhacén's west flank to join and follow the Río Mulhacén to Refugio Poqueira. Then go down the well-marked trail past Cortijo de Las Tomas that enters Barranco de Poqueira, and hence to Central Electricá, Cebadilla and Capileira (5hr 30min).

5   To the ski area: descend Mulhacén's west flank to Refugio de la Caldera. Pick up the old road and follow it to Collado de Carihuela, round the western flanks of Veleta and down to Hoya de la Mora (3hr 30min).

ROUTE 28
Round of the northern peaks via Peña Partida

Start/Finish	Trailhead, Vereda de la Estrella
Alternative start/finish	Trailhead, Loma de los Cuartos
Distance	37km; from alternative start: 22km
Total ascent	2490m; from alternative start: 1110m
Grade	Tough; from alternative start: challenging
Time	15hr/2–3 days; from alternative start: 10hr 30min/2 days
Summits	Picón de Jérez, Puntal de Juntillas, Tajos Negros de Cobatillas, Puntal de los Cuartos, Pico de la Justicia o Atalaya, Pico del Cuervo, Puntal de Vacares
Water sources	Río Vadillo, spring at Peña Partida, Lavaderos de la Reina
Seasonal notes	In winter this makes a fine hillwalking circuit. In July and August a better start would be via car to Loma de los Cuartos (see below), giving higher access to Refugio Forestal Peña Partida.

This is a fine tour for lovers of solitude and wild places. The northern peaks may not have the dramatic faces of the giants further south, but there is a special quality to the walking here. This multi-day trek visits the delightful Lavaderos de la Reina valley before ascending the ring of 3000m peaks above.

Potential camping spots are available at Peña Partida, Lavaderos de la Reina, Cuneta de Vacares and Laguna de Vacares.

Alternative start from Loma de los Cuartos

From the trailhead, where a chain across the road indicates where cars must be left, it's a gentle 2hr walk east over the sub peak of **Papeles** (2424m) to **Refugio Peña Partida**. Keep to the ridge crest where an easily followed path leads the way. Don't be tempted by the longer dirt road running down to the left (north).

Leave the car park and cross the bridge. Turn left onto the 'Vereda de la Estrella' path and follow it for 3km to a signpost and junction of paths. At the junction of paths go left down the hill to cross the Río Genil near the ruined **Refugio Vadillo** at Puente de los Burros. The track now climbs up **Cuesta de los Presidiarios** to approach **Refugio Forestal La Cucaracha** at 1750m (2hr, 6.5km).

Refugio Peña Partida, with views south to Veleta

From Picón de Jérez a party can be seen ascending the easy slopes of Tajos Negros de Cobatillas

Just before the refuge, keep on the Loma del Calvario path rather than turning right to the refuge. After 10min and at about 1900m take a path off to the left, which follows an irrigation channel north east towards the Río Vadillo. Cross the **river**. The path makes a series of sweeping turns as it ascends to **Refugio Forestal Peña Partida** at 2440m (4hr, 12km).

> **Peña Partida** is a fine refuge, restored in 2015 and situated near some rocks a few kilometres east of the rounded summit of Papeles (2424m). It has superb vistas south to the Sierra Nevada, covering the peaks from Picón de Jerez right through to Veleta. It is especially pleasant to sit and watch the sun set over Granada from here.
>
> A small natural **spring** 300m south east of the refuge at the upper end of Barranco de Peña Partida (below the level of the refuge) is sometimes the only water source around here, unless you're prepared to walk into the Lavaderos de la Reina.

Take the path behind the refuge that goes east, rising gently for 1.5km to reach the wide valley of **Lavaderos de la Reina**. Drop into and cross the valley, passing right (south) of the small peak of **Cerro de Poco Trigo** (2688m), to reach a confluence of streams and rivers by a **waterfall**.

> The best time to visit **Lavaderos de la Reina** is in the spring when the hillsides are teeming with streams, waterfalls and snowmelt.

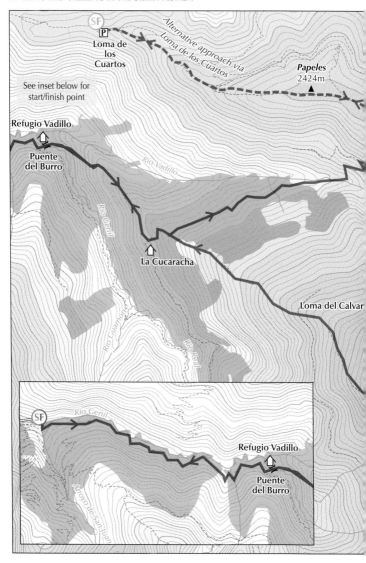

N

0   1
km

Refugio Forestal
Peña Partida

Cerro de
Poco Trigo
2688m

Picón de Jérez
3090m

Lavaderos de la Reina

Tajos Negros
de Cobatillas

Alternative route back
to Peña Partida
and Loma de los
Cuartos trailhead

Puntal
de Juntillas
3139m

Puntal de los Cuartos
3158m

Cerro del
Mojón Alto

Pico de la
Justica o Atalaya
3135m

Río Trevelez

ntal de
s Negros

Collado de las Buitreras

Pico del Cuervo
3144m

Collado de Vacares

Laguna de
Vacares

Puntal de Vacares
3136m

191

From here it's a 1hr 30min and 450m climb to Picón de Jérez, which rises across the scree hillside to the east. Cross the stream and climb alongside the waterfall until the ground eases. There are some faint paths but they are hard to follow; the natural line of the land takes you north east and then east direct to the summit cairn of **Picón de Jérez** at 3090m (7hr, 17km). This is the first 3000m summit on the main ridge line of the Sierra Nevada.

It's an easy 1km hands-in-pockets stroll south west to **Puntal de Juntillas** (3139m), with more and more of the view to the south opening up ahead. The path continues west around the upper rim of Lavaderos de la Reina to the next peaks, **Tajos Negros de Cobatillas** (3116m) and **Puntal de los Cuartos** (3158m; 8hr, 19.5km).

Alternative return to Loma de los Cuartos

If you've parked at the Loma de los Cuartos trailhead, it's better to return from this point using the broad north west ridge of Puntal de los Cuartos to descend to **Refugio Peña Partida** (9hr, 17.5km) and hence easily back to the trailhead.

To continue on the main route, go south over **Pico de la Justicia o Atalaya** (3135m) to **Pico del Cuervo** (3144m; 9hr 15min, 21km). (The descent into the pass of **Collado de las Buitreras** from Atalaya might need some care in mist or snow as the rocks of the ridge line can't be followed in their entirety. The slopes to the left (east) always provide the easier solution. There is a steep pull from the col up to Pico del Cuervo.)

If desired, it would be a simple matter to pick up the peaks of **Cerro del Mojón Alto** (3107m) a short distance to the north, and **Puntal de Tajos Negros** (2983m) to its west, and then retrace steps to the main route.

From Pico del Cuervo, continue south down the ridge towards Puntal de Vacares. The ridge narrows, and some turns left and right of it are made on the way down to the pass of **Collado de Vacares**.

Just west of Collado de Vacares is a small shallow valley that makes a convenient place to camp. This is called **Cuneta de Vacares**. Snow seems to linger longer here than elsewhere. If no water is available then the only option would be to drop down east from the pass to Laguna de Vacares.

Laguna de Vacares is one of the Sierra Nevada's deepest lakes. It holds many superstitions for local people – in particular the legend of the bird-woman. She is said to have appeared to travellers as a beautiful woman who spoke kind words of love but ultimately deceived and drowned them.

The Laguna and Puntal de Vacares

According to locals, anyone who sees her will inevitably be doomed. The superstitious may prefer to camp at Collado de Vacares!

There are paths on both sides of the ridge leading to Puntal de Vacares; that to the right is easier than the one of the left, which requires some simple scrambling on loose ground. Further on, the ridge broadens and leads to the summit of **Puntal de Vacares** (3136m; 10hr 30min, 23km). This is a fine viewpoint – especially towards the impregnable-looking wall of the north face of Alcazaba. Having enjoyed the view, retrace steps to **Collado de Vacares**.

The route now descends, initially north then north west, on an old drovers' trail called the Vereda de la Laguna de Vacares. Although not always easy to follow in its upper reaches, after 1.5km and 150m of descent a better path leads easily enough to the junction with **Loma del Calvario**. Here a faint path may or may not be encountered, but it hardly matters – the way down the broad ridge is obvious. Aim for the left edge of a forest 350m below, where a decent track is found.

Continue down the ridge of Cuesta de los Presidiarios to cross the **Río Genil** by Puente del Burro (14hr, 32.5km). After a short climb back up to the Vereda de Estrella, follow this back to the start. The long descent from the col may mean your knees will be buckling a bit by the time the nearest bar and welcome drink is found!

JÉREZ DEL MARQUESADO
AND REFUGIO POSTERO ALTO

The easy angled slopes around the upper bowl of Barranco del Alhorí (Photo: Felipe Nieto Conejero) (Route 29)

The town of Jérez de Marquesado lies at the foot of the most northerly 3000m peak of the Sierra Nevada, Picón de Jérez. A path south of the town gives access to only the second guarded refuge of the range, Refugio Postero Alto – notable as the usual start-point for the epic Los Tres Miles Integral (Route 31).

There are some small rural guest houses and apartments to rent in the town itself, but most visitors will come from Granada (70km) or Guadix (17km).

Getting to Jérez del Marquesado
Jérez del Marquesado is located 15km south of the busy city of Guadix. The easiest approach is via the A-92 south of Guadix, leaving the motorway at km303. Join the N-324 towards Guadix and after 3km turn left onto the GR-5104, signposted Jérez del Marquesado (30min).

Getting to Refugio Postero Alto
The drive to Refugio Postero Alto takes a further 45min. The refuge is situated on a firebreak above Jérez del Marquesado on the main route to Picón de Jérez. The

road to the refuge from the town was upgraded in 2016 and saloon cars can now be taken to the refuge. The last few kilometers are a bit rough but if this deters, there are places to park the car before this section.

Take the main road through Jérez del Marquesado towards Lanteira. Just after leaving the main town, turn right on a tarmac road signposted 'Refugio Postero Alto'. At km1, just past the Centro Contraincendios buildings, turn left on a wide forest road. At km12 leave the forest road (signed Refugio Postero Alto; cars can be left here if necessary) and turn right, rising more steeply on a deteriorating track. Reach the refuge at km14. Cars can be parked and left here.

There is a useful service offering transfers from Jérez del Marquesado to the refuge in 4WD vehicles – contact details can be found on the refuge website: www.refugioposteroalto.es/traslados-en-4x4/

The walk to Refugio Postero Alto (3hr)
If the access road to the refuge is closed due to snow, it is possible to walk from the town. Just after leaving the main town, ignore the tarmac road on the right (signposted 'Refugio Postero Alto') and continue some 400m until a road veers off to the right. Take this, and after 100m branch left on a dirt track, which materialises into a path after 1km. The well-signposted route crosses a river and rises steadily just left of the ridge line to reach the refuge.

ROUTE 29
Ascent of Picón de Jérez and round of the Alhorí valley

Start/Finish	Refugio Postero Alto
Distance	16km
Total ascent	1330m
Grade	Tough
Time	8hr
Summits	Picón de Jérez, Puntal de Juntillas, Cerro Pelao, Piedra de los Ladrones
Water sources	Barranco del Alhórí
Seasonal notes	The winter season here can be quite busy – especially at weekends – as Barranco del Alhórí is a popular mountaineering destination among locals, with many fine routes.

Picón de Jérez is the most northerly 3000m peak in the Sierra Nevada. This ascent, via Barranco del Alhóri, is the finest way to the summit and is followed by a high-level walk round the rim of the valley with an optional ascent of Cerro Pelao.

Follow the firebreak south west from Refugio Postero Alto. Take note of the broad hillside opposite – Loma de Enmedio – as this is used for the return journey from the summits. After just under 1km, turn right and follow the path alongside the forest edge as it wends its way into the Arroyo del Alhóri river valley.

> The river valley can retain large **snow** patches until late spring or even early summer, and it may be necessary to bypass these rather than risk a fall through the soft melting snow into the tunnel that normally lies beneath.

The path steepens as it ascends initially left (south) of the riverbed. Higher up it crosses to the northern bank as it approaches the spectacular cirque of cliffs comprising **Barranco del Alhóri** (2hr 30min, 5.5km)

After 700m of ascent, the base of the cirque itself makes a welcome and convenient place for a rest stop. From here the remainder of the route can now be seen: above the cliffs is Piedra de los Ladrones and to its right Puntal de Juntillas; further right and rising to the north west is Picón de Jérez.

Route around the Barranco del Alhórí ascending the Picón de Jérez

Cerro Pelao
Puntal de Juntillas
Picón de Jérez
Piedra de los Ladrones
to Puerto de Trevélez
Barranco de Alhori
Refugio Postero Alto

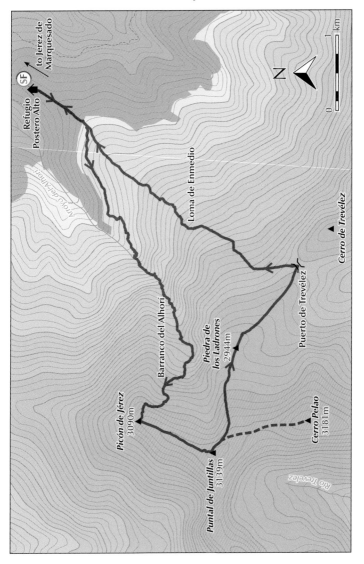

It's a further 500m of ascent to the summit. Follow the path as it makes a turn to the north before heading again west. It's a straightforward but relentless ascent until the summit of **Picón de Jérez** is gained (3090m; 4hr 30min, 7.5km).

There are widespread **views** from the top of Picón de Jérez. To the east the vast valley of Lavaderos de la Reina is spread out below, with Granada away in the distance. However, it's the southern aspect that catches the eye, with a line of peaks and ridges leading to the dominant Alcazaba and the bulk of Mulhacén lurking behind. Away to the south west, Veleta and Cerro de los Machos are prominent.

The hard work has been done and the route now becomes much easier. **Puntal de Juntillas** (3139m) is a straightforward 1km south along a nearly level path. From there the route turns and descends gradually eastwards, following the rim of the crags of Barranco del Alhorí towards **Piedra de los Ladrones** (2944m).

Optional ascent of Cerro Pelao
An easy addition from Puntal de Juntillas, for those keen to pick up an extra 3000m peak, would be to walk south for 1.5km to the summit of **Cerro Pelao** (3181m) – a peak often overlooked but in a fine situation at the head of the Trevélez valley. It's well worth the mere 90m of ascent involved and adds only an hour. Return the same way, but at the col you can traverse right to join the descent path to **Piedra de los Ladrones**.

Puerto de Trevélez lies not far below. It's an easy walk to reach the **pass** (6hr, 11.5km), where a path on the right joins from the Trevélez valley. Turn left and begin the 900m of descent on the broad slopes of **Loma de Enmedio**, eventually returning to **Refugio Postero Alto**.

View south from Picón de Jérez

PUERTO DE LA RAGUA

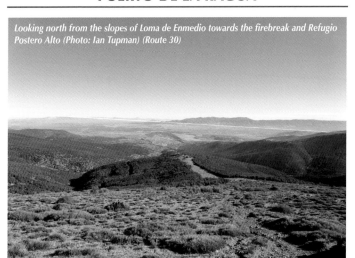

Looking north from the slopes of Loma de Enmedio towards the firebreak and Refugio Postero Alto (Photo: Ian Tupman) (Route 30)

Puerto de la Ragua is a high road pass (2000m) that cuts through the eastern Sierra Nevada between La Calahorra in the north and the villages of Bayárcal and Laroles in the eastern Alpujarras to the south. A network of cross-country ski tracks spreads out from the pass, making it a popular place for school parties who come to enjoy the sledging and snowshoeing in winter.

The pass makes a good high start-point for the gentler terrain of the eastern Sierra Nevada. There's a car park, an *albergue*/hostel sleeping 32 and a restaurant. You can find up-to-date information about Puerto de la Ragua, snow and access conditions by visiting www.puertodelaragua.com

Getting to Puerto de la Ragua

Access is easiest from the north via Guadix, the A92 and the town of La Calahorra. Turn left in the town onto the A-337, signposted 'Puerto de la Ragua'. The road climbs up towards the pass. There are some narrow sections, so great care should be taken on meeting other cars. Signs will indicate if the road is affected by snow and ice. Chains may be necessary. (13km, 25min from La Calahorra.)

ROUTE 30

The eastern peaks

Start	Puerto de la Ragua
Finish	Refugio Postero Alto
Distance	26km
Total ascent	1510m
Grade	Challenging
Time	9hr, 2 days
Summits	Morrón del Hornillo, Morrón Sanjuanero, Morrón del Mediodía, Alto de San Juan, Peñón del Lobo, Piedras de Pelegrina, Peñón del Puerto, Puerto de Jérez, Cerro de Trevélez
Water sources	Very little between Puerto de la Ragua and Puerto de Trevélez. The heads of sheltered southern valleys offer the most likely places to camp, with possible springs south of Piedras de Pelegrina, Peñón del Puerto, Collado del Puerto and Puerto de Trevélez.
Seasonal notes	Good winter hillwalking terrain, but the ridge is open and exposed to the winds.

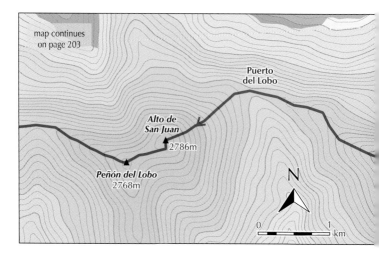

map continues on page 203

Puerto del Lobo

Alto de San Juan
2786m

Peñón del Lobo
2768m

N

0 1 km

This trek can be used as an add-on to the Integral de Los Tres Miles (Route 31) but makes a rewarding excursion in its own right. It covers the high ground east of Puerto de Trevélez and entails two days of fairly straightforward walking over high, undulating, rolling hills.

Camping is possible at many places along the ridge but finding water in the summer months will be the main problem.

From the car park at Puerto de la Ragua, cross the road and head south west up the wide firebreak in-between the forest edges. Either continue following the line of the valley bottom as it swings round to the west, or take to the slightly steeper but more direct slopes on the left. Either way, the broad upper slopes of **Morrón del Hornillo** (2375m) are soon reached (45min).

Ascend via the broad ridge to the south west; it's easy strolling, steepening towards the summit of **Morrón Sanjuanero** (2610m; 1hr 30min, 4km).

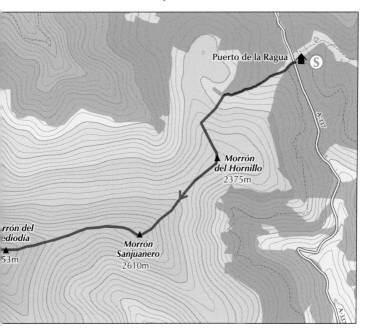

201

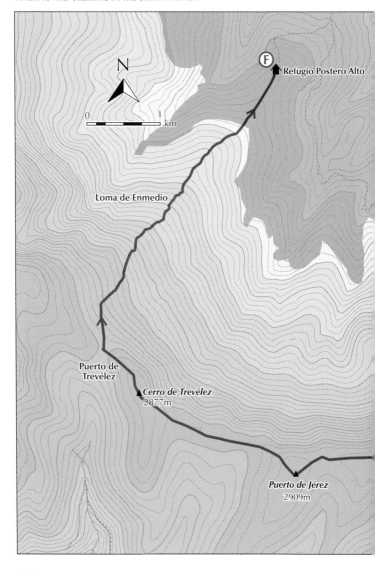

The ascent to Morrón Sanjuanero

Collado del
Puerto

Peñón del Puerto
2754m

Piedras de
Pelegrina
2609m

Looking east from Puerto de Trevélez gives an idea of the nature of this walk: long distances over high, exposed but relatively straightforward mountains (Photo: Ian Tupman)

Far away in the distance to the west, the first 3000m peak of the Sierra Nevada – **Picón de Jerez** – can be seen. It's a sobering thought that the end of this walk at Refugio Postero Alto is just this side of that peak. A long distance to be covered over undulating hill country!

The next summit to the west, **Morrón del Mediodía** (2753m) is a fairly easy 2km away. Morrón del Mediodía has some steep cliffs to its north that give entertaining but straightforward winter mountaineering routes. From there the ridge drops gently to **Puerto del Lobo** (2400m) – where in adverse weather a long escape is possible by descending either to the north (Aldeire, La Calahorra) or south (Válor, Alpujarras) – and then from Puerto del Lobo a steep 300m re-ascent of a broad ridge leads to **Alto de San Juan** (2786m; 3hr 30min, 10km).

Between Alto de San Juan and Cerro de Trevélez there is 10km of undulating ridge with no major climbing involved. The route passes over the summits of **Peñón del Lobo** (2768m), **Piedras de Pelegrina** (2609m), **Peñón del Puerto** (2754m; 5hr, 14km) and **Puerto del Jérez**. Again, in bad weather, escape from the ridge can be made at the col of **Collado del Puerto**, just west of Peñón del Puerto. (It would be much quicker to head north down to Lanteira rather than south to Berchules.)

From the summit of **Cerro de Trevélez** (2877m), make the short and easy descent north west for 500m to the pass of **Puerto de Trevélez** (7hr, 21km), where a path on the left joins from the Trevélez valley. To hook up with the Tres Miles Integral (Route 31), continue north west from the col towards the next peak, Piedra de los Ladrones. Turn right and begin the 900m of descent down the broad slopes of **Loma de Enmedio** to **Refugio Postero Alto**.

MAIN RIDGE TRAVERSE
AND LONGER TREKS

Sunrise at Collado de Carihuela, with the Tajos de la Virgen ridge and Cerro de Caballo in the background (Route 31)

Getting to Refugio Postero Alto

Refugio Postero Alto, which underwent some major restoration work in 2010, is the start-point for Route 31. It is situated on a firebreak above Jérez del Marquesado on the main route to Picón de Jérez. The drive is initially along tarmac road, then forest track and finally by rough track. The road to the refuge from the town was upgraded in 2016 and saloon cars can now be taken to the refuge. The last few kilometers are a bit rough but if this deters, there are places to park the car before this section.

Take the main road through Jérez del Marquesado towards Lanteira. Just after leaving the main town, turn right on a tarmac road signposted 'Refugio Postero Alto'. At km1, just past the Centro Contraincendios buildings, turn left on a wide forest road. At km12 leave the forest road (signed Refugio Postero Alto; cars can be left here if necessary) and turn right, rising more steeply on a deteriorating track. Reach the refuge at km14. Cars can be parked and left here (45min).

There is a useful service offering transfers from Jérez del Marquesado to the refuge in 4WD vehicles – contact details can be found on the refuge website: www.refugioposteroalto.es/traslados-en-4x4/

If the access road to the refuge is closed due to snow, it is possible to walk from Jérez del Marquesado: just after leaving the main town, ignore the tarmac road on the right signposted 'Refugio Postero Alto' and continue some 400m further to take a road veering off to the right. After 100m branch left on a dirt track, which becomes a path after 1km. The well-signposted route crosses a river and rises steadily just left of the ridge line to reach the refuge (850m, 3hr).

Getting to Hoya de la Mora

Hoya de la Mora is the start-point for Route 32.

From the main Granada ring road (Circunvalación), follow the well-signposted mountain road to Sierra Nevada (A-395). This leads to the main ski resort at Pradollano. At km30, just before entering the resort, turn left following signs to Hoya de la Mora and Albergues de Granada. At km35 and 2500m altitude the road ends and there are car parks on either side. This is Hoya de la Mora. Snow chains may be necessary if the road has not been cleared.

Getting to El Dornajo

The Centro de Visitantes Dornajo (a Sierra Nevada National Park visitor centre) is the suggested start-point for Route 33 – although the route may be joined at any convenient point.

By car from the main Granada ring road (Circunvalación), follow the well-signposted mountain road towards the Sierra Nevada (A-395). El Dornajo is on a sharp bend in the road after 25km, just after passing Restaurant El Desvío on the left (25min).

Autocares Tocina (www.autocarestocina.es) run a daily bus service between Granada and the ski area, dropping off at El Dornajo. Many more buses operate in the winter ski season than throughout the rest of the year.

ROUTE 31
'Los Tres Miles' Integral 3000m peaks

Start	Refugio Postero Alto
Alternative start	Puerto de la Ragua
Finish	Lanjarón
Distance	65km; from Puerto de la Ragua: 89km
Total ascent	3470m; from Puerto de la Ragua: 5370m
Total descent	4730m
Grade	Very tough
Time	3–5 days; from Puerto de la Ragua: 5–7 days
Summits	Noted in route description
Water sources	Noted in route description
Seasonal notes	Between November and May this is a major winter mountaineering expedition suitable only for those experienced in high-altitude winter alpine environments. Spring trekkers should be aware that the northern slopes of Alcazaba and around Veleta, Paso de los Machos and Tajos de la Virgen can contain snow into June and crampons may well be necessary. A mid-summer descent to Lanjarón will be uncomfortable due to the heat, so an early-morning start is recommended.

The ultimate multi-day trek of the Sierra Nevada, covering all the major 3000m peaks in the range. It can be done in either direction, but north to south is the traditional way, as described here.

For non-mountaineers the trek is usually doable from mid May until mid November, but this does depend on late- or early-season snowfall. It will take between three and five days in high summer, with some delectable overnight camping places by mountain streams or lakes. Additional water may have to be carried during the day in the summer months of July, August and September, until the next water source is located.

The length and roughness of the terrain north of Alcazaba should not be underestimated. This section brings the most arduous underfoot conditions, with some faint trails and paths. Arriving on Mulhacén to be met by the summer hordes will provide a shock. From Veleta southwards, normal service is resumed and there will be fewer people on the quieter mountain tracks.

Potential camping sites with reliable water sources are to be found at Barranco del Alhóri, Laguna de Juntillas, Laguna de Vacares, Lagunas de las Calderetas, Barranco de Goterón, Cañada de Siete Lagunas, Laguna de la Caldera, Lagunas de Río Seco, Lagunas de Aguas Verdes, Laguna de Lanjarón and Laguna de Caballo.

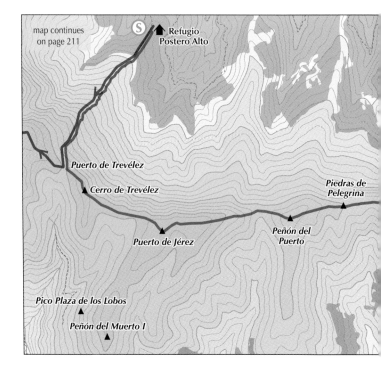

The ultimate Integral – a two-day extension

This two-day extension to Los Tres Miles starts from the pass of Puerto de la Ragua, which is accessed via the town of La Calahorra, and extends westwards to Puntal de Juntillas, where the main route is joined. It adds two days of fairly straightforward but high-level walking onto the original trek. For a more detailed description of this extension, see Route 30.

From the car park at the pass, cross the road and head south west up the wide firebreak in-between the forest. Either continue following the line of the valley bottom as it swings round to the west, or take to the slightly steeper and more direct slopes on the left. Either way, the broad upper slopes of **Morrón del Hornillo** (2375m) are soon reached.

Ascend to **Morrón Sanjuanero** (2610m) via the broad ridge opposite. From there the ridge undulates all the way to Puerto de Trevélez, going over the summits of **Morrón del Mediodía** (2753m), **Alto de San Juan** (2786m), **Peñón del Lobo**

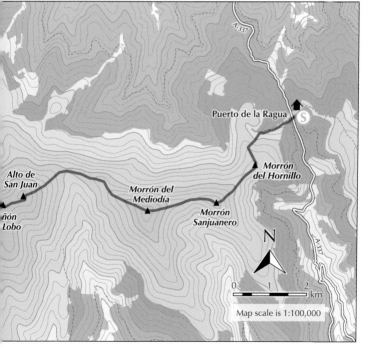

(2768m), **Piedras de Pelegrina** (2609m), **Peñón del Puerto** (2754m), **Puerto de Jerez** and finally **Cerro de Trevélez** (2877m).

From the summit of the Cerro de Trevélez descend north west for 500m to **Puerto de Trevélez**. The easy angled slopes north west of the pass lead to the sub-peak of Piedra de los Ladrones on the rim of Barranco del Alhóri; follow the escarpment west from here to reach **Puntal de Juntillas** (3139m). If you're a purist you'll want to bag the peak of Picón de Jerez to the north. Pick up the main Integral route.

The main route from Refugio Postero Alto

Follow the firebreak south west from Refugio Postero Alto. Turn right along the forest edge and follow the path towards the river. Continue on the northern bank of the river to enter below the spectacular cirque of cliffs comprising Barranco del Alhóri.

Go up towards the head of the valley before making a turn to the north and heading to the summit of **Picón de Jerez** (3090m, 7.5km). From here it's an easy 1km south to **Puntal de Juntillas** (3139m). The extension joins the main route here. (If you're intent on bagging all of the 3000m peaks, don't forget **Cerro Pelao**

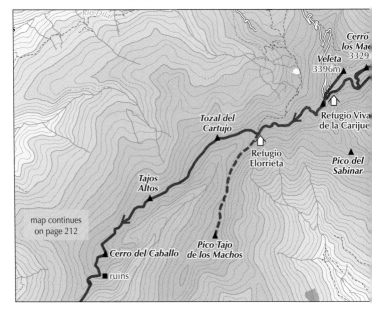

map continues on page 212

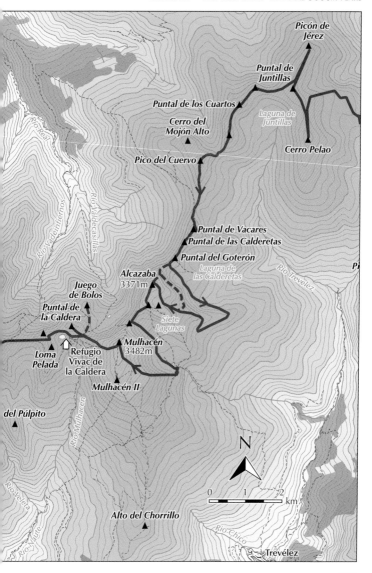

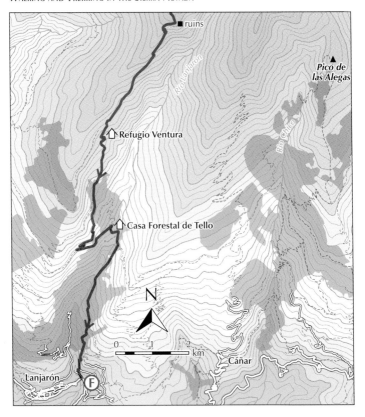

(3181m) to the south.) Water is available just south west of Puntal at Laguna de Juntillas.

Continue west around the upper rim of Lavaderos de la Reina to the next peaks, Tajos Negros de Cobatillas (3116m) and **Puntal de los Cuartos** (3158m), before turning south over Pico de la Justicia or Atalaya (3135m, 13.5km). From Atalaya, the descent into the pass of Collado de las Buitreras might need some care in mist or snow as the rocks of the ridge line cannot be followed in their entirety. The slopes to the left (east) always provide the easier solution. This is followed by a steep pull up to **Pico del Cuervo**, 14km. Purists may wish to pick up the peak of Cerro del Mojón Alto (3107m) a short distance to the north.

From Pico del Cuervo continue south down the ridge towards Puntal de Vacares. The ridge narrows, and some turns to the left and right of it are made on the way down to the pass of Collado de Vacares.

> Just west of Collado de Vacares is a small, shallow valley that makes a convenient place to **camp**. Snow seems to linger longer here than elsewhere. If no water is available, the only option would be to drop east from the pass to Laguna de Vacares.

There are paths on both sides of the ridge leading to **Puntal de Vacares**; that to the right is easier than the left, which requires some simple scrambling on loose ground. Above, the ridge broadens and leads to the summit (3136m, 16km). This is a fine viewpoint – especially towards the impregnable-looking wall of the north face of Alcazaba.

The character of the ridge changes as you head south west from Puntal de Vacares and over **Puntal de las Calderetas** (3066m). It features big blocks and rocky pinnacles which are easy enough to circumnavigate, although care should be taken – particularly on snow and ice.

Sunrise on Alcazaba from Lagunas de las Calderetas

There is a potential **campsite** with water at Lagunas de las Calderetas 150m down to the east: the easiest approach is to follow the south east ridge of Puntal de Vacares and lower down traverse back south west to the lakes. This is arguably one of the finest places to spend the night in the whole range.

Once past Puntal de las Calderetas the going is much easier to **Puntal de El Goterón** (3067m).

In the upper Goterón valley lies some of the **wreckage** of a DC-6 aircraft that crashed there in 1964. It is rumoured that the passengers were fairly well off and a few weeks after the crash, some of the locals in Trevélez were seen walking around the village wearing expensive shoes and coats!

To get from Puntal del Goterón to the summit of Alcazaba (3371m) there are a few options. The simplest and best in poor weather is to follow the path south east into Barranco de Goterón and cross the river at 2820m. From here the path rises gently to cross the eastern shoulder of Alcazaba at 2850m, where a large prominent pinnacle called 'Piedra del Yunque' marks the path leading onwards to Siete Lagunas; our route, however, leaves that path and climbs the east ridge. From Piedra del Yunque it's 2.5km and a tough 550m ascent to the summit cairn of **Alcazaba** (23km).

Ascent of Alcazaba via Paso de las Zetas

This option involves some potentially complicated route-finding over loose and stony terrain, but it's 1hr 30min quicker and 2.5km shorter than the route via Piedra del Yunque.

From Puntal del Goterón take a faint path leading up and under the crags of Tajos de Goterón. The path goes south west below the line of imposing overhanging crags and materialises into a better path lower down as it cuts through a section of cliff. Here the path is lost somewhat in scree and boulder slopes, but the key is to keep rising slowly, traversing these slopes to where a green horizontal line cuts through some low crags. At this point some cairns are met and the route from here on is easy. Follow the path as it climbs up the scree to the base of the crag, then follow an obvious rising shelf from bottom left to top right to reach the col above. A large cairn marks the top of Paso de las Zetas; turn right and follow the broad ridge to the summit of **Alcazaba**.

The summit of Alcazaba in late spring (Photo: Felipe Nieto Conejero)

Cutting through the low crags to Paso de las Zetas on Alcazaba

Ascent of Alcazaba via Cañuto Norte de Alcazaba
This is a rough and loose scramble **not to be recommended with a heavy pack**. It saves 2hr, 4km and 200m over the main route.

Above Puntal de Goterón a track leads to the right along a shelf – the Gran Vasar de Alcazaba. Don't take this. Instead continue on to the second shelf above, named Cuneta de Alcazaba. Turn right along this and follow it to the first major wide gully coming down from the summit. This is Cañuto Norte de Alcazaba. Turn left and climb the rough, loose ground to the summit of **Alcazaba**. Some scrambling moves are involved.

The next section between Alcazaba and Puntal de Siete Lagunas can be a bit complicated. The path south of Alcazaba runs just below the ridge crest but it's simple to pick up the peak of Puntal de la Cornisa (3307m) and Peñon del Globo (3279m) at the southern side of the upper plateau. A prominent cairn just down and east of here marks the start of the descent of El Colaero – a steep scree gully cutting down between the crags directly to the upper lakes of Siete Lagunas.

There is no scrambling in the El Colaero gully, but it is loose and steep. At half-height and just below a rocky section of the path a move right (there may be faint tracks) under the base of the crags can be made towards the ridge. Continue

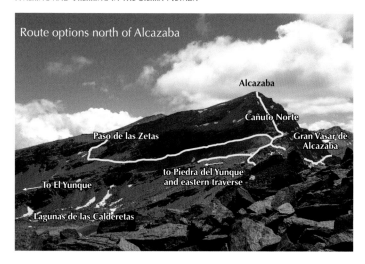

Route options north of Alcazaba

Alcazaba

Cañuto Norte

Paso de las Zetas

Gran Vasar de Alcazaba

to Piedra del Yunque and eastern traverse

To El Yunque

Lagunas de las Calderetas

traversing east under the rocks until a short climb leads back up to reach the pass and Puntal de Siete Lagunas (3244m, 24.5km).

It's possible from here to climb up the north east face of Mulhacén via a combination of sliding scree gullies and blocky, boulder-strewn ridges – but this is not to be recommended with a heavy multi-day backpack. The safest course of action is to drop down to Siete Lagunas.

Follow the path from Puntal de Siete Lagunas as it descends steeply, zig-zagging east through the screes. It's not long before the base of the valley and Laguna Hondera are reached (26km). Ample camping sites and water are available here.

From Laguna Hondera at **Siete Lagunas** a well-marked path zig-zags up the steep hillside south of the lake to reach a small col, where a large cairn marks the spot at which the eastern traverse path joins. Follow the ridge ahead as it rises then curves round to the right towards the summit. Small cairns mark the track, which is faint in places. There is sometimes a choice of path; in mist or under snow keep the escarpment on your right-hand side until the broader slopes of the upper mountain are reached and the track coming up from Mirador de Trevélez to the south is joined. Turn right and follow the easy slopes to the summit of **Mulhacén** at 3482m (29km).

Descend the west flank of Mulhacén to the col, Collado del Ciervo, and from there scramble up the south east ridge of **Puntal de la Caldera** (3323m), either taking scrambling sections direct or bypassing them to the south. Return to the pass the same way and then go south west to **Refugio Vivac de la Caldera**, or head directly to the refuge via the steep scree slope south of the summit. A campsite and water are available near the lake.

The peak of Juego de Bolos lies north of the Collado del Ciervo and strictly speaking this is one of the 3000m peaks, however few make the journey there and back (2hr 15min extra).

Take the path that traverses the hillside behind the refuge and above the lake to a col just 100m south of Puntal de Laguna Larga (3178m). From there descend on the path to join up with the old road near Crestones de Río Seco.

Most people don't include the numerous points of the jagged and broken **Crestones de Río Seco** in their 'Integral'. However, there's a campsite and water at Lagunas de Río Seco just below and south of the road.

Follow the road for 2.5km until below Cerro de los Machos. From the junction of paths just beyond Paso de los Machos, turn right to ascend to **Cerro de los Machos** (3329m, 36km). The only safe and straightforward way off this is to follow the broad ridge south west; take the path just left of the first pinnacle on the Las

Camping in Cañada de Siete Lagunas, with the crags of Alcazaba rising behind

Campanitas ridge, which leads easily down to the old road just west of Paso de Los Machos, 25min from the summit.

Take a path veering away to the right a few metres after the junction with the old road. This leads round the south western bowl of Veleta to arrive very quickly at a short section of chain-assisted track. This is the Paso de las Guías – simple but exposed. (If the thought of the chain-assisted route doesn't appeal then it's a simple matter to just keep to the old road.) Once through it's only 10min to rejoin the old road and reach the Carihuela **refuge** and col (38km).

Ascend **Veleta** (3394m) from the col, following the edge of the escarpment northwards for the best views. Afterwards return same way to the pass.

To reach Refugio Elorrieta from Collado de Carihuela there are two options: a straightforward route via the winter ski run (see alternative route below), or a crossing of the Tajos de la Virgen ridge that requires some scrambling and is at times exposed.

To tackle the ridge, start by climbing Puntal de Loma Pua (3234m) (many parties bypass this on the right-hand side and gain the ridge beyond). From here follow the delightful ridge crest, which is interspersed with easy rocky sections. After 30min a rock tower (3228m) blocks the way; climb easily up the tower until 20m below the top, then traverse slanting ledges in an exposed situation on the right-hand side. This is followed by easier going on a broader ridge.

Pass left of a rocky 20m-high gendarme known as the Fraile de Capileira, and make a descending traverse to the col before another rock step (3191m) bars the way. Take a traverse line left for 50m before climbing right back up a narrow rake to the ridge line, above the step. From here the ruined **Refugio Elorrieta** (3160m) is easily attained via a blocky ridge (42.5km).

> Strictly speaking, the 3000m peaks are not completed without the peak of **Tajo de los Machos** (3085m); however, this is 3km away to the south, making a 6km return journey from the refuge. Tajo de los Machos is a fine mountain but few will bother with it and it remains only for the purists!

The high ridge to Cerro del Caballo is tackled next. The initial way west from Refugio Elorrieta is untracked but crosses a stony plateau aiming for the ridge opposite that will lead to Tozal del Cartujo. The path is faint in places, with small cairns indicating the route. At one point on the ridge crest there is an awkward step down, followed immediately at a cairn by a short traverse down on the western (right) side of the ridge. In front a large cliff bars the way but is easily avoided by a path to the left, which then ascends easily to **Tozal del Cartujo** (3152m, 44km).

The journey south west from here is obvious, although tracks are sometimes faint. Don't be tempted to avoid the summit of **Tajos Altos** (2987m) by a flanking path, as it's a fine summit in its own right.

> On the main ridge line at a col just 500m south west of Tajos Altos, some level ground provides a good **camping site** – or there's a substantial cave in the rocks close by (but no water in the summer). It's a fantastic situation to watch the setting sun over the Vega de Granada, and one of the best campsites on the main ridge.

Continue over the summit of **Cerro del Caballo** (3005m, 49.5km) which lies some 2km away over an undulating ridge, and round the bowl south of the peak to arrive, 4hr after Refugio Elorrieta, at the **ruins** just after Hoya del Zorro.

To get to Refugio Ventura the best advice in good weather is to stick to the long south ridge until nearly above the refuge, where a direct pathless descent can be made to the *acequia* (irrigation channel) above it. (In poor weather the path traversing the hillside east of this ridge is safer; the path is well-marked and leads to the same place.)

At the **refuge** (2250m, 53.5km) you might be forgiven for thinking that the bulk of the journey had been completed, but there remains some 1600m of unremitting descent.

A path leads past the refuge and within 15min arrives at a dirt road. Your next objective is **Casa Forestal de Tello** – some white painted buildings set next to the Río Lanjarón at 1700m. The route down to these ruins changed dramatically after a major wildfire in September 2005, and in 2017 maps still didn't reflect the route accurately. However, the 'new' route is quite obvious – although there are a variety of options. The infallible guide in any difficulties is to follow the dirt road until you're above an obvious helipad by another dirt road. Paths drop down to this and the dirt track can be followed initially north east before coming back south east to the ruins.

Below Tello, cross the **Río Lanjarón** and take the well-signposted drovers' path (Camino de las Sierras) that follows the eastern bank of the river to the town of **Lanjarón**. From Lanjarón there are regular buses to Granada and onwards to Guadix/Jerez de Marquesado (**www.alsa.es/en**).

ROUTE 32
'Los Tres Picos' – Veleta, Mulhacén and Alcazaba

Start	Hoya de la Mora
Finish	Trevélez
Distance	48km
Total ascent	2910m
Total descent	3920m
Grade	Tough
Time	3 days
Summits	Veleta, Mulhacén, Mulhacen II, Alcazaba
Water sources	Río Seco, Río Mulhacén, Laguna de la Caldera, Siete Lagunas
Seasonal notes	A superb route in winter. Technical difficulties are low but there may be avalanche risk below Cerro de los Machos and the eastern traverse of Mulhacén. The west flank of Mulhacén gets heavily iced in early winter. Be prepared to change plan accordingly. Straightforward high-altitude hiking in summer.

There are many ways to cover the three highest peaks of the Sierra Nevada in a three-day trek; this is one of the best that doesn't involve wild camping. It spends two nights at Refugio Poqueira, allowing light and fast travel during the day. The route described is linear, starting above the ski area and finishing in Trevélez.

The 'Tres Picos, Sierra Nevada' has become a popular charity fund-raising challenge, especially during May, June, September and October.

There are many possible variations to Los Tres Picos. Camping out is more aesthetically pleasing than staying at the refuge, with less height loss each day, but involves carrying more weight. Numerous suitable camping sites but the major ones would be at Laguna de Rio Seco, Laguna de la Caldera and Siete Lagunas.

A start and end at Capileira would also be possible, thus saving the need for use of public transport, a second car or a friendly driver.

Veleta from Hoya de la Mora

Day 1 Veleta (3394m) – 900m ascent, 16km, 7hr 30min

From Hoya de la Mora, ascend the broad northern slopes of Veleta on a variety of well-marked tracks that pass either side of the Virgen de las Nieves statue and left of the Telesilla de la Virgen chairlift station. There are plenty of options, but the best stays away from the ski detritus and old road and keeps the escarpment edge of Barranco de San Juan to the left. The ascent to the 3100m northern shoulder of Veleta, named **Posiciones del Veleta**, should take just less than 2hr.

From the summit of Veleta there are superb views east to Mulhacén and Alcazaba

There are three options for reaching the summit from here: you can either keep as close to the edge of the ridge as possible as it curves leftwards to the summit (this requires a head for heights and some scrambling ability); or you can stay on the old road as it traverses west of the summit, gaining height gradually and looking out for a path near a ski sign for 'Descenso Hombres' that leads uphill through the scree to the left, then joining the ridge crest higher up to the left and following it to the summit (this makes for a more interesting ascent – although it is just a walk, with no scrambling nor a head for heights required); or thirdly you could continue on the old road until it splits, and then take the left branch which meanders and zig-zags up the gentle south west face of the mountain to easily reach the summit of **Veleta** (3hr 30min, 7km).

Head south from the summit to the pass of **Collado de Carihuela**, then follow the old road east past Paso de los Machos to the head of the Río Seco valley, south and below the jagged rocky crest of the Crestones de Río Seco ridge (4hr 45min, 10km). Drop down to the eastern lake at **Lagunas de Río Seco**, descending faint tracks at the head of the Río Seco, east of the jagged ridge of Raspones de Río Seco. Contour round the southern shoulder of Loma Pelada to reach **Refugio Poqueira**.

Day 2 Mulhacén (3482m) – 1000m ascent, 10km, 5hr 30min

From the refuge, follow the trail north west as it gradually descends to join the **Río Mulhacén**. Paths ascend both sides of

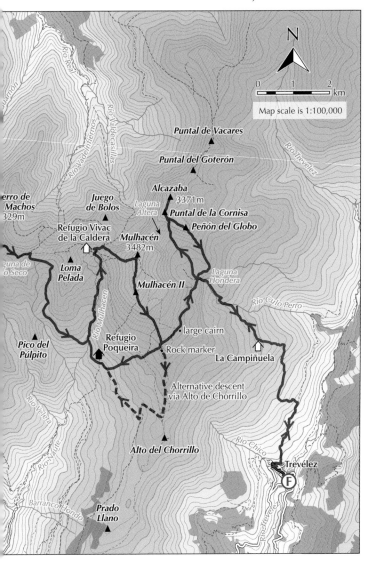

223

the river, but the path to its west is perhaps preferable; follow this to a junction with the old road, passing through some delightful *borreguiles* (high-mountain meadows) in its upper reaches.

The west flank of Mulhacén towers above you. Here there are a few options, but our route takes the well-cairned path from the old road some 300m south east of **Refugio Vivac de la Caldera** (2hr, 4km). Just follow the interminable zig-zag path as it climbs the 450 vertical metres to the summit of **Mulhacén**. The path seems never-ending but in fact 1hr 30mins or less will see you on the top (3hr 30min, 5km).

To return to Refugio Poqueira, follow an easy path south towards Mulhacén II. Just before the south summit, ignore the semblance of a road that turns off eastwards and pass just left of the summit cairn. Take the path that descends just west of the ridge line into a shallow bowl, which you traverse.

Follow the path as it switches to the east of the ridge line and descends to the 3000m level, where you meet an old road coming in from the east. At a corner of the road and junction of the Mulhacén path you will see 'Mulhacén' and '7 Lagunas' markers painted on a **rock**; at this point take a faint path south west and down some scree to cross the old trans-Sierra Nevada road before dropping down a shallow gully to a dirt road. Turn right to reach the **refuge**.

Alternative descent via Alto de Chorrillo

A longer (by 1hr and 3km) but safer descent from the painted **rock marker** in mist or poor conditions is to continue down the main, well-cairned path to **Alto de Chorrillo**. From here a signposted dirt road leads to the **refuge** without difficulty.

Day 3 Alcazaba (3364m) – 1000m ascent, 22km, 9hr 30min

An early start from the hut is required as this is likely to be the toughest day. Head south east on the well-marked dirt road up to the junction with the old road at Alta del Chorrillo, and then start up the south ridge of Mulhacén (45min, 3km).

At 3000m, white lettering painted on a rock on the right of the path points to '7 Lagunas' – the next objective. Instead of following the path up the south ridge of Mulhacén, take the old road towards Siete Lagunas as it climbs gently, trending north eastwards onto the open plateau. About 700m after the sign on the rocks, you'll come to two large cairns; these signify the start of the eastern traverse of Mulhacén to Siete Lagunas (1hr 45min, 6km).

Leave the road and follow the track on the right. The path trends northwards, contouring the hillside and around valleys, but generally descending until it joins the path coming down from the east ridge of Mulhacén at a large cairn. A few metres further on, start the short but steep descent north to **Laguna Hondera** – the biggest lake at Siete Lagunas (2hr 30min, 8km). Cañada de Siete

Alcazaba from the north – arguably the finest of Los Tres Picos

Lagunas is a beautiful and tranquil spot consisting of seven lakes in a dramatic mountain setting.

From Laguna Hondera, walk up the gently graded valley floor, passing alongside tumbling streams and tranquil lakes and aiming for the upper centre of the valley. There are some faint tracks but the way is obvious up to the upper basin, where the highest lake, **Laguna Altera**, lies encircled by cliffs and ridges.

Just before reaching the lake, take a track heading north east up the steepening and rocky slopes, aiming for an obvious col between Puntal de la Cornisa (3307m) and Peñón del Globo (3279m). There are cairns marking the way, and although the ascent is steep and loose it is without difficulty. (At one point a hand may be useful to continue upward progress, but this could hardly be called scrambling.) The col is marked by a large cairn and is reached sooner than expected. Make a note of this spot for the return journey or in misty conditions.

Ahead lies the fairly level plateau area leading to the summit. Take the good path that continues round the rim of the valley just below the ridge crest before climbing to the large cairn on the summit of **Alcazaba** at 3371m (5hr, 10.5km).

The simplest descent – especially in mist – is to return the same way to **Siete Lagunas** (6hr 30min, 13.5km). The path to Trevélez starts from the lip of the corrie where the **Chorreras Negras** waterfall tumbles over the lip; it's a well-trodden route down from here to cross the Río Culo Perro and then continue to Trevélez via the emergengy shelter of **La Campiñuela**. Allow 3hr from Siete Lagunas. From Trevélez there are buses to Granada (**www.alsa.es.en**) and to Hoya de la Mora (**www.autocarestocina.es**).

ROUTE 33
The Sulayr GR240

Start/Finish	Centro de Visitantes Dornajo (Sierra Nevada National Park Visitor Centre, Dornajo)
Distance	302km
Total ascent	10,071m
Total descent	9213m
Grade	Tough
Time	15–20 days
Water sources	Sufficient throughout most sections of the walk but a filter is useful, especially in summer and autumn
Seasonal notes	In midwinter snow may affect this walk, but the snow levels are generally higher – except on the northern sections around Postero Alto and Peña Partida when the snows could last until mid May.

Sulayr – the 'Mountains of the Sun', as the Arabs used to call the Sierra Nevada – has given its name to a 300km footpath (the GR240) that encircles the range. It is divided into 19 sections that cover tens of kilometers of old traditional paths, animal tracks and cattle routes. The path was inaugurated in November 2007 and is designed to help walkers link small villages at about the 2000m level around the Sierra Nevada, getting a flavour along the way of past Arab and Andalucian cultures and influences.

The walk can be done as a whole or in selected day-sections. In its entirety, it usually takes between 15 and 20 days. There is a lot of flexibility on this trek for longer or shorter days, or for side-excursions into the Sierra Nevada en route. Wild camping is recommended, as is the use of basic mountain shelters. Of course, the start doesn't have to be made at the Centro de Visitantes El Dornajo; the trek can be started wherever is most convenient.

Possibly the best section of the route is in the north from La Roza westwards to Dornajo through the Postero Alto and Peña Partida sections. The least interesting sections are arguably in the south east, from Lastonar through to El Cerecillo where long stretches of dirt road snaking in and out of valleys become rather tedious.

Waymarking is in the form of wooden posts bearing the classic red-and-white horizontal bands and the name GR240. Above this a logo of the emblematic plant of the Sierra Nevada, the *estrella de las nieves*, with a circle representing the circular nature of the footpath. It's worth pointing out that the waymarking assumes a clockwise direction of travel – some difficulties may be encountered if travelling anti-clockwise.

It is not the intention of this guide to give a detailed description of the route (which is probably worth a whole guidebook for itself!); the following sections will, however, give some idea of what's involved and may help in planning.

Section 1 – Centro de Visitantes El Dornajo to Casa Forestal La Cortijuela
4–5hr, 14.5km, 610m ascent, 570m descent
The route starts off heading south west through woodlands on a dirt road, slowly descending to cross the Río Monachil. Then comes the hardest part of the day: a 500m ascent towards Cerro del Mirador. A pleasant traverse west towards Pico del Tesoro is followed by a gentle descent through forests to Casa Forestal La Cortijuela.

Section 2 – Casa Forestal La Cortijuela to Rinconada de Nigüelas
5–6hr, 19.5km, 1240m ascent, 580m descent
This day involves the most ascent of any on the Sulayr; it's an arduous day that includes many valley-crossings. It starts with a slow climb on forest roads to Collado de Chaquetas before crossing the Río Dílar and ascending steeply to cross Loma de Peñamadura. After crossing the Río Durcal, good dirt roads are picked up in order to navigate the lower western flanks of Cerro de Caballo and reach the mirador at the Rinconada.

Section 3 – Rinconada de Nigüelas to Tello
4–5hr, 15km, 160m ascent, 600m descent
A very simple day's walking on high dirt roads. The route crosses the south western and southern slopes of Cerro de Caballo before entering the Río Lanjarón valley.

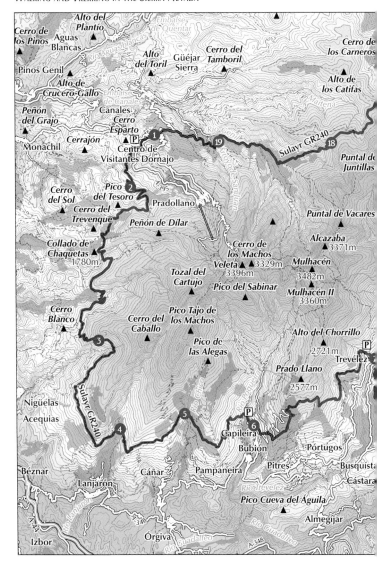

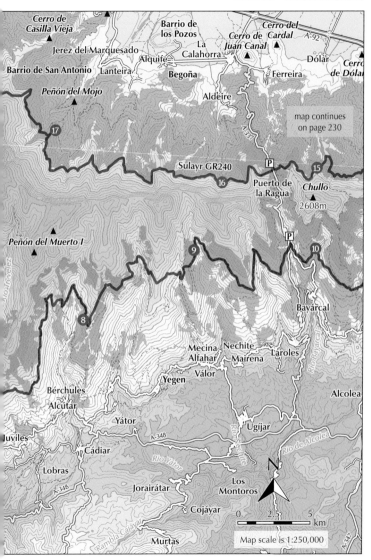

map continues on page 230

229

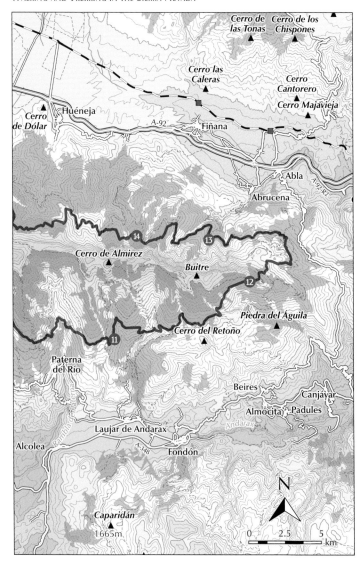

Forest trail through the western Alpujarra

Section 4 – Tello to Puente Palo
3–4hr, 8.5km, 410m ascent, 210m descent
Another straightforward day moving east on high dirt roads to access the forested area at Puente Palo.

Section 5 – Puente Palo to Capileira
4–5hr, 10.5km, 510m ascent
An interesting day, initially gaining height by following the Acequia de Almiar to cross a low shoulder of Las Alegas, where the white villages of the Alpujarra, backed by Mulhacén, come into view. This is followed by a descent on a combination of dirt road and good tracks to cross the Río Poqueira by the Puente Chiscar, before the gentle climb up to the village of Capileira.

Section 6 – Capileira to Trevélez
5–7hr, 17.5km, 920m ascent, 920m descent
A hard day with a lot of ascent, crossing the lower southern slopes of Mulhacén. The *barrancos* (gorges) of Cerezo and Chorrea precede Hoya del Portillo, and the high point of the day is reached near Prado de las Juncias before a long cross-country descent leads to the dirt road near Barranco de la Bina. Easy thereafter to the village of Trevélez.

Section 7 – Trevélez to Lastonar
7–8hr, 25km, 970m ascent, 570m descent
One of the toughest days on the circuit. Fortunately the major ascent comes at the start of the day as the climb is made to El Portichuelo. The descent to Hoya

Herrera is short-lived before a seemingly endless dirt road eventually drops to cross the Río Grande and take you uphill to the finish.

Section 8 – Lastonar to Fuente del Espino
5–6hr, 16.5km, 340m ascent, 490m descent
The route follows a combination of tracks and dirt roads weaving in and out of valleys, crossing streams and slowly descending to the Fuente.

Section 9 – Fuente del Espino to Barranco Riachuelo
5–7hr, 20.5km, 330m ascent, 470m descent
A long but relatively easy section over low mountain shoulders and around valleys on gently angled tracks. The highlight of the day is the steep drop into and out of the Arroyo del Palancón valley south of Puerto de la Ragua.

Section 10 – Barranco Riachuelo to El Cerecillo
5–6hr, 15km, 540m ascent, 500m descent
A relatively straightforward leg, crossing the shoulder of Hoya de los Carmones before a long descent into the Río Paterna valley. This is followed by a short ascent of Loma de Majada de Vacas and on to the end.

Near Peña Partida, looking south to the Sierra Nevada giants of Alcazaba and Mulhacén

Section 11 – El Cerecillo to La Polarda
7–8hr, 20.5km, 930m ascent, 610m descent

This section is notable as El Polarda sits at the most easterly end of the Sulayr. The route crosses Barranco del Horcajo easily enough and then the path drops steeply to cross Barranco del Palomar. Next is the hardest part of the day: an 800m climb in 7km to reach the Sierra Nevada ridge line at La Polarda near Collado del Espino. A tough day but rewarding day.

Section 12 – La Polarda to La Roza
4–5hr, 17km, 190m ascent, 880m descent

A very enjoyable and easy section, with the path turning westwards along the northern flanks of the Sierra Nevada. It's mainly downhill, hands-in-pocket strolling to Loma de Atalayuela and Venta de Serbal and onto La Roza, accompanied by some great views of the surprisingly rocky mountains of Berro del Buitre and Peña Horadada.

Section 13 – La Roza to Piedra Negra
3–4hr, 13km, 720m ascent, 60m descent

A short day, but mainly uphill as the route continues west over Barranco de Peña Horadada and up to Cuerda de Limones. Again, superb views of some of the lesser-known peaks of the eastern Sierra Nevada.

Section 14 – Piedra Negra to El Toril
5–6hr, 18.5km, 470m ascent, 480m descent

This section, heading west, crosses many rivers and valleys, sometimes on forest roads and sometimes on good trails. A straightforward yet interesting day.

Section 15 – El Toril to Las Chorreras
3–4hr, 11km, 140m ascent, 280m descent

A very easy day with minimal ascent, the route crosses the road pass of Puerto de la Ragua and Barranco de los Passilos.

Section 16 – Las Chorreras to Postero Alto
7hr, 21.5km, 570m ascent, 550m descent

Although the ascent on this section is not severe, the distance is. The route crosses countless rivers, valleys and high moorland using trails and forest roads. Ahead looms the Picón de Jérez, the first 3000m peak of the Sierra Nevada. At its base is the chance to ditch the tent for a night and stay at the welcoming Refugio Postero Alto.

Section 17 Postero Alto to Peña Partida
5–6hr, 16km, 660m ascent, 130m descent

This is a day spent mainly in ascent as the route from the refuge crosses over the northern shoulder of Picón de Jérez to enter the high valley of Lavaderos de la Reina – a wonderful place to be, especially in the spring. The scenery more than makes up for the effort involved; this is one of the best sections of the Sulayr and should not be missed. The walk ends at the Peña Partida refuge with its superb views to the main Sierra Nevada mountains.

Section 18 – Peña Partida to La Hortichuela
5–6hr, 14km, 90m ascent, 1220m descent

In contrast to the previous section, this one is characterized by descent. The route drops to and crosses the Rio Vadillo and Río Genil, and continues along the Vereda de Estrella before a short rise at the end leads to Cortijo de la Hortichuela.

Section 19 – La Hortichuela to Centro de Visitantes Dornajo
2–3hr, 7km, 440m ascent, 100m descent

This last section up to El Dornajo might seem a bit of an anticlimax after all the splendours of the Sulayr so far. It's an easy half-day walk – perhaps for the best after previous exertions!

HIGH MOUNTAIN
SCRAMBLES

Near the summit of Puntal de la Caldera (Route 35)

The following provides a selection of some of the best scrambles in the Sierra Nevada mountains for those in search of adventure or an adrenaline rush. There are five scrambles in all – three on ridges and two up buttresses. It is not a definitive list; there is plenty of opportunity here for further exploration and for finding new routes.

A helmet, harness and rope are advised for security on all of the high mountain scrambles. All become major winter mountaineering routes under snow and ice (at grades PD+ to AD+).

ROUTE 34
Espolón de Alcazaba

Start	Junction of Espolón and the Gran Vasar de Alcazaba
Finish	Alcazaba summit
Total ascent	350m scrambling
Grade	3S
Time	1hr 30min–2hr scrambling
Summits	Alcazaba
Approach	From Alto de Chorrillo (3hr 30min) via Collado del Ciervo

The steep north west face of Alcazaba presents the scrambler with few opportunities, but the Espolón is a classic tough scrambling route in a big mountain environment. It is 'Alpine' in feel and in nature.

Be warned, though: it is the hardest scramble in this guide both in terms of technical difficulty and seriousness. It involves sustained 3S scrambling and difficult route finding. Any deviation from the easiest line up the buttresses will land you on more technical terrain with few escape options.

Approach
Access to the face is most easily made from **Collado del Ciervo**, near Laguna de la Caldera and west of Mulhacén summit, which can be reached from Alto de Chorrillo (which is accessible by bus or on foot) in 2hr. Take the zig-zag path leading down into the northern corrie of Mulhacén, where the picturesque **Laguna de la Mosca** sits (2hr 45min from Alto de Chorrillo).

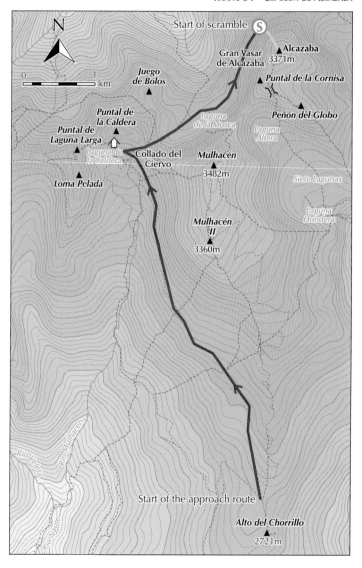

N

0   1
└────────┘ km

Start of scramble ⓢ

Gran Vasar
de Alcazaba

▲ Alcazaba
3371m

Juego
de Bolos
▲

Puntal de la Cornisa ▲

Laguna
de la Mosca

Peñón del Globo ▲

Laguna
Altera

Puntal de
la Caldera
▲

Puntal de
Laguna Larga
▲

Laguna de
la Caldera

Collado del
Ciervo

Mulhacén
▲
3482m

Siete Lagunas

Loma Pelada
▲

Laguna
Hondera

Mulhacén
II
▲
3360m

Río Veleta

Río Mulhacén

Río Naute

Start of the approach route

Alto del Chorrillo
▲
2721m

237

Just a short distance north of the lake take a faint path which trends right and then gains an obvious sloping shelf that crosses the face of Alcazaba. This is called the **Gran Vasar de Alcazaba** (3hr 30min).

The next task is to identify the start of the Espolón – which is easier said than done as steep rock and crags abound everywhere. These are some features to look out for, though. Look down and try to follow the obvious ridge line coming up from the valley below. Where it joins the Gran Vasar should be the start, on a large flat platform. The continuation of the Vasar path to the pass north of Alcazaba can be seen in its entirety; above you there should be a steep and quite intimidating wall of rock. An identifying feature is a vein of white quartz that runs horizontally across this wall about 30m up from the platform.

The route
When you actually get to grips with the rock the steepness relents, good holds are found and the climb progresses. The initial buttress is overcome surprisingly easily by a variety of devious means, always searching for the easiest line. It will concentrate the mind and you certainly won't be thinking of work or how to pay the next mortgage bill!

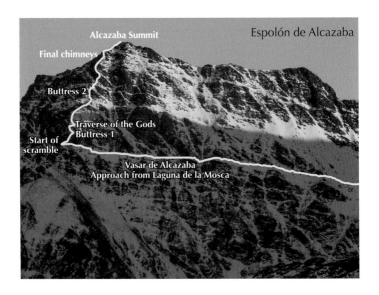

238

The start of the 'Traverse of the Gods'

At the top of the initial 50m and after climbing a leftward-sloping gully, it seems an impasse is reached. Here a spectacular traverse rightwards is required: a Sierra Nevada-style 'Traverse of the Gods'. It is very exposed and you certainly don't want to fall here, but the holds are large and comforting. A rope may be sensible for those of a nervous disposition, and a couple of intermediate belays will be easily found if required.

Above this the scrambling continues. Cross a scree ledge and go up the second part of the initial buttress. The trick here is to keep trending to the right and not be tempted off to the left. At the top of the initial buttress there's a short walk along the ridge before crossing some loose scree; here the second buttress is met.

After the excitement of the initial pitches, the scrambling on the second buttress has a slightly more relaxed feel to it. It's open and enjoyable, although you may have to search around for the easiest line.

The final rocks can be climbed via a series of easy but 'thrutchy' chimneys (or even avoided entirely on the right if necessary) before the final ascent to the summit of **Alcazaba** (3371m), the finest peak in the Sierra Nevada mountain range.

Descent

From the summit, follow the rim of the escarpment southwards on a good path to the col between Puntal de la Cornisa and Peñón del Globo. A large cairn here marks the start of 'El Colaero' – a wide scree gully which drops down to Laguna Altera. A well-marked trail leads easily onwards to Laguna Hondera. From there a path traversing round the eastern side of Mulhacén joins the south ridge of Mulhacén at 3000m and hence to Alto de Chorrillo (3hr 15min from Alcazaba summit).

ROUTE 35
Traverse of Puntal de la Caldera

Start	Puntal de Laguna Larga
Finish	Collado del Ciervo
Total ascent	150m scrambling
Grade	2
Time	1hr 30min scrambling
Summits	Puntal de Laguna Larga, Puntal de la Caldera
Approach	From Posiciones del Veleta (2hr) via Col de Carihuela; from Alto de Chorrillo (2hr)

The west-to-east traverse of Puntal de la Caldera gives fine high-altitude scrambling. It has the feel of a big-mountain route and certainly features some fine moments. Some route-finding choices which contribute to a wholly entertaining and enjoyable experience.

Approaches
- In summer an approach can be made from the north by catching the first chairlift or bus from the ski area to Posiciones del Veleta. This will save the walk in from Hoya de la Mora. Swift progress can then be made on the old road over Collado de Carihuela and on to the start at the summit of **Puntal de Laguna Larga**.
- From the south, take the summer bus service from the National Park Information Office in Capileira to Alto de Chorrillo, and then walk to **Refugio de la Caldera** before traversing easily to **Puntal de Laguna Larga**.

The route
The ridge heads eastwards in a convoluted and chaotic manner towards Puntal de la Caldera. It is characterized by some solid sections of rock on the ridge crests,

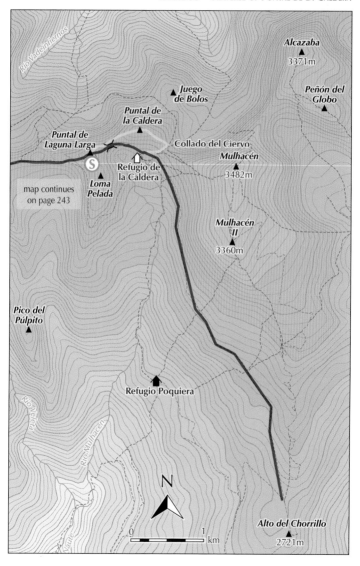

map continues
on page 243

On the ridge shortly after leaving Puntal de Laguna Larga

Puntal de
la Caldera

West ridge Puntal de la Caldera

Espolón de la Caldera
upper Buttress

Harder alternative

Crux traverse through boulders
left of large cliff

Best
scrambling

Small col

Easy alternative
to reach col

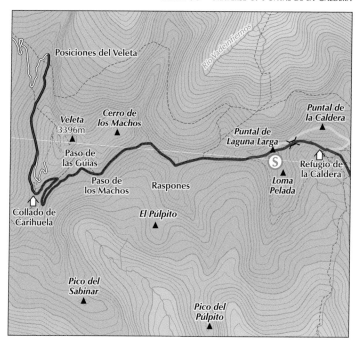

but if the crest is deviated from, a combination of steep ground and loose rock will be encountered.

It is immediately apparent that a huge crag bars the route halfway along the ridge in front of you; this will form the crux section later in the scramble. The initial going on the ridge is straightforward; try to keep to the crest for maximum scrambling. It's easy enough, with some nice Grade 2 sections if you like. There are a couple of moments where the best option is to be bold (both in ascent and descent), with a brief raising of the standard to Grade 3. This is preferable to the tactic of avoidance – usually to the right, which appears easier but will likely see you on loose rock.

Just before reaching the col before the large crag, you'll come to some pinnacles. They lead to an exposed 3m downclimb, or a slightly easier chimney just before and to the right. (To avoid this whole section, retrace your steps to before the pinnacles and drop down a loose scree shelf to the left (north).)

From the col before the large crag, the best scrambling route trends leftwards up a ramp formed by huge boulders. This leads to an initial gully, which can be climbed rightwards to the ridge crest at Grade 3. The easiest line is to keep trending left up rising ground on slabby rock with small but superb in-cut holds. There are many variations here, all of Grade 1/2 standard.

Gain the ridge crest and continue to the summit (3223m), linking as many of the rock outcrops as you wish. Harder options abound if you prefer!

The descent of the east ridge to the col, **Collado del Ciervo**, is easy (Grade 1). Keep to the ridge crest for maximum enjoyment rather than being tempted to take avoiding action. Ahead of you rises the impressive north wall of Mulhacén, with Alcazaba to its left.

Descent

At the Collado del Ciervo turn right and it's a 10min walk to **Refugio de la Caldera** and the regular walking tracks. From the refuge it's 1hr 15min to **Alto de Chorrillo** and 2hr 15min to Posiciones del Veleta.

ROUTE 36
Espolón de la Caldera

Start	Base of ridge 10min east of Laguna Larga
Finish	Collado del Ciervo
Total ascent	350m scrambling
Grade	3
Time	2hr scrambling
Summits	Puntal de la Caldera
Approach	From Posiciones del Veleta (3hr) via Collado de Carihuela; from Alto de Chorrillo (3hr 15min) via Collado del Ciervo

The Espolón de la Caldera is in fact the north west ridge of Puntal de la Caldera, found just to the west of Collado del Ciervo. It gives a rough and sometimes loose scramble, with many possibilities for making the ascent easier or tougher to suit. The route is difficult (and dangerous) to descend or escape from due to the loose nature of many of its sections.

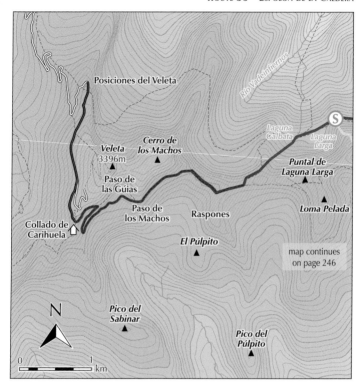

Approaches

- From the south, take the summer bus service from the National Park Information Office in Capileira to Alto de Chorrillo, and then walk up to **Collado del Ciervo** (2hr). Drop down north from the col and almost immediately take a faint path leading down towards Juego de Bolos and around the northern side of **Puntal de la Caldera**. Cross a wide gully and traverse along a rocky buttress to the start (3hr 15min).

- In summer an approach can be made from the west by catching the first chairlift or bus from the ski area to Posiciones del Veleta. This will save the walk in from Hoya de la Mora. Swift progress can then be made on the old road over **Collado de Carihuela**, **Paso de las Guías** and **Paso de los Machos**. After passing through the cutting of the Raspones ridge, look for a cairn on

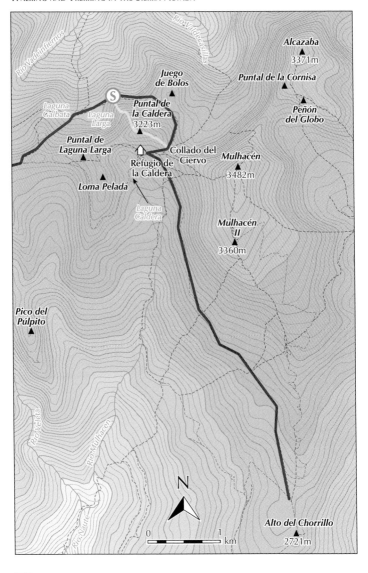

Espolón de la Caldera

Mulhacén

Puntal de la Caldera

Upper buttress

Escape rake right to
Puntal de la Loma Pelada

Loose middle section

Initial easy ground

Laguna Large

the left. Go up to the col, cross over the main ridge and follow the steep path down to **Lagunas Larga** and **Galbata**. It's a 10min easy walk from Laguna Larga to the start, where the path cuts across the base of the ridge. The start of the actual route will become apparent as height is gained.

The route

Keep Laguna Larga in sight on the initial ascent of the ridge and if easier alternatives are required, move further east. It's easy 'hands-in-pockets' going for the first 15min up gently sloping slabs, and then the first pinnacles are met. The rock is quite solid around here, so don't be too tempted to take easier (and looser) routes off to the left. Take the rock buttresses head-on for the most enjoyment.

A level section gives time for a short rest, with superb views back down to the Lagunas and across to Cerro de los Machos. Above, things start to look tougher.

The middle section of the climb is quite clearly on poorer rock. Yellow, broken rock abounds here. Test each hold carefully, especially if taken direct. Escape is possible to the left but will put you on some exposed and loose terrain.

Above the middle section, at a short col, an escape can be made to the right along a faint goat track to reach the west ridge coming from Puntal de Laguna Larga, but this would detract from the quality of the finishing line leading to the summit.

Puntal de la Caldera

Espolón de la Caldera – upper sections

Upper buttress

Loose middle section

Some fine sections of good rock provide excellent scrambling opportunities

The upper section is on much better rock, so be bold and enjoy the airy and spectacular surroundings. As you top out onto the summit ridge the southern side of the Sierra Nevada comes into view with Laguna de la Caldera far below you.

The descent of the east ridge to the col, **Collado del Ciervo**, is easy scrambling (Grade 1). Keep to the ridge crest for maximum enjoyment rather than being tempted to take avoiding action.

Descent
At the Collado del Ciervo turn right and it's a 10min walk to **Refugio de la Caldera** and the regular walking tracks. From the refuge it's 1hr 15min to **Alto de Chorrillo** and 2hr 15min to Posiciones del Veleta.

ROUTE 37
Arista de las Campanitas

Start	Cerro de los Machos (3329m)
Finish	Veleta (3394m)
Total ascent	300m scrambling
Grade	2/3
Time	1hr 30min scrambling
Summits	Cerro de los Machos, Zacatín, Campanario, Salón, Veleta
Approach	From Posiciones del Veleta (1hr 30min) via Corral del Veleta or Collado de Carihuela

A superb round of the Corral del Veleta, including the summits of Cerro de los Machos (3329m), Zacatín (3307m), Campanario (3318m), Salón (3325m) and Veleta (3394m). The airy and spectacular sections look hard but are on mainly good rock so the confident scrambler will gain most benefit.

Approach
The best approach is to use the summer bus from Hoya de la Mora to **Posiciones del Veleta**. Drop into and cross the **Coral de Veleta** (30min) and then head up the scree slopes to the col just west of Cerro de los Machos.

Las Campanitas ridge leading from Cerro de los Machos to Veleta
(Photo: Ian Tupman)

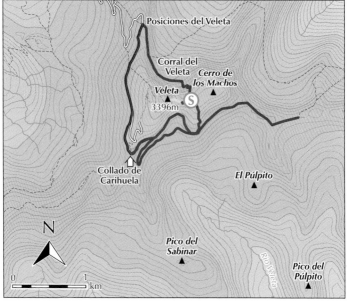

Alternatively the same point can be accessed using the old road, passing through **Collado de Carihuela** and then taking the path on the left immediately before Paso de los Machos.

The route

From the summit of **Cerro de los Machos** the obvious ridge of Las Campanitas lies to the west. Walk west along the broad ridge to the start of the first rocky

251

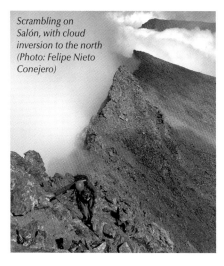

Scrambling on Salón, with cloud inversion to the north (Photo: Felipe Nieto Conejero)

rise to Zacatín. Here keep to the ridge crest for maximum enjoyment; it's simple Grade 1 stuff and just a sample of the superb delights to follow.

After descending to the col between Zacatín and Campanario, things appear decidedly more difficult and a bold approach is required. The west ridge of Campanario rises like a needle into the sky – a magnificent sight. The wise will don helmets here as the scrambling level goes up a notch. The way is slightly to the left of the ridge (the alternative to the right being overhanging!), following a line marked by the passage of others. A cool head is needed as it is steep, but there are superb 'thank God' holds to assist upward progress.

The exposure eases at the summit of Campanario. Make an easy descent just left of the ridge to the next col before Salón. At this col there are signs of tracks to left and right; the safest way is to pass to the right here on the less loose alternative. Rise easily on the northern side to another small col, then traverse upwards and left in a series of small steps to gain the col between Salón and Veleta. The savage cleft of Canuto del Veleta drops steeply down on the right here – it's a popular winter mountaineering route (PD+/AD-) and has even been skied!

A direct ascent of Veleta from the col is out of the question; instead traverse some 40m horizontally south on a vague path. The orange letters '1FF' marked on a rock signify the start of Fidel Fierro, the route to the summit.

It is similar scrambling to that on Campanario: some steep rocky sections mixed with scree ledges. Follow the route as it rises until below the summit ruin and then cuts through a short gully and ends up on the summit of **Veleta**.

Descent

From the summit, many well-marked paths lead south or west to join the old road between **Collado de Carihuela** and **Posiciones del Veleta**.

ROUTE 38

North ridge of Tozal del Cartujo

Start	Base of the north ridge beyond Laguna Misterioso
Finish	Tozal del Cartujo summit
Total ascent	300m scrambling
Grade	3
Time	2hr scrambling
Summits	Pico del Tozal del Cartujo
Approach	From Hoya de la Mora (3hr) via Collado de las Yeguas

A long and sustained scramble up a fine ridge, reminiscent of the Cuillin of Skye, that ends on the summit of Tozal del Cartujo. The described route is Grade 3, but the grade lowers to 2 if all difficulties are avoided. At the other end of the scale, if the ridge is adhered to throughout then a short abseil and a 20m climb of HVD is required.

Approach
Follow Route 23 past Borreguiles to **Collado de las Yeguas** (1hr 30min). Once over the col, drop steeply south west before traversing undulating slopes and trending uphill to the fabulous lake of **Laguna Misterioso** (2680m). A faint track and scattered cairns mark the way to the lake (2hr 30min).

> **Laguna Misterioso** is well-named, as it's tucked away in a secluded valley surrounded by towering cliffs.

The ridge appears close from here but is a frustrating 30min further across boulder fields, scree slopes and shallow valleys – always trending uphill towards the obvious start of the ridge.

The route
There is no obvious start; it's a broad, easy ridge that can be walked up with hands in pockets. As you gain height the ridge narrows and some rock steps start to appear. The start of the scrambling becomes apparent.

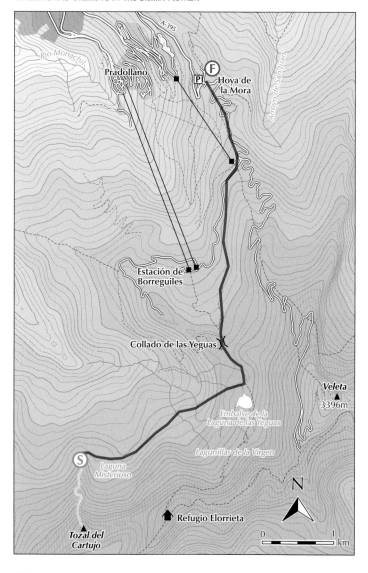

North ridge, Tozal de Cartujo

Easy upper ridge

Easy angled scrambling back to crest

Rock climbing section

Bypass round base of cliffs

Leave main ridge

Best scrambling

All rock on the ridge crest could initially be avoided on scree to the right, but these rock ridges, cracks and walls prove to be quite entertaining and give a sample of the delights to come.

North ridge, Cartujo – bypass

Ridge left here

Low angled easy scramble leads back to ridge east

Bypass round base of cliffs

The route takes the chimney on the right and is much easier than it looks!

With the exposure increasing, follow some narrow sections of ridge until the ridge abuts against a huge cliff face which bars the way. Just to the right, though, is an obvious gully providing the key to the next section. Ascend the gully; it is steep but with good holds throughout.

Emerge onto the crest and continue along the ridge and over a small tower until the remainder of the route to the summit comes into view. Ahead lies a complex mass of rock towers; you will now have to leave the ridge in order to avoid a short 10m abseil followed by a 20m rock climbing pitch of about HVD.

The avoiding route takes a line down steep scree to the right and contours around the base of the next buttress and into the gully beyond. Don't take the first main gully up as it will bring you to the col between the abseil and the rock pitch. Instead, traverse across the gully to gain some easy angled rock slabs beyond. Turn left and follow these up (some Grade 1 moves), alternating between the rock and some steep, loose scree to regain the ridge south of the rock pitch.

Turn right and continue along the ridge. All scrambling sections can be avoided again by easier alternatives to the right. Eventually emerge on the gently sloping summit plateau that leads to the summit of **Tozal del Cartujo** (3152m).

Descent

Descend north east from the summit, avoiding the cliff by a well-marked path on the right to join the ridge to Refugio Forestal Elorrieta. Then go down to Lagunillas de la Virgen to join the approach route at **Collado de las Yeguas**. Retrace steps back to the start.

APPENDIX A
List of the 3000m peaks

Name	Height (m)	Grid reference	Route number
Mulhacén	3482	723 008	2, 5, 6, 27, 31, 32
Veleta	3394	675 012	21, 31, 32, 37
Alcazaba	3371	732 024	1, 31, 32, 34
Mulhacén II (Alcazaba)	3361	723 998	2, 5, 6, 32
Cerro de los Machos	3329	681 013	22, 31, 37
Puntal de la Cornisa	3307	729 019	31
Peñón del Globo (Alcazaba)	3279	735 016	31
Puntal de Siete Lagunas	3244	726 014	8, 31
Tajos de la Virgen	3228	664 001	21, 31
Puntal de Loma Pua	3224	670 003	34, 42
Puntal de la Caldera	3223	709 013	7, 31, 35, 36
Puntal de Laguna Larga	3181	703 010	7, 31, 35
Cerro Pelao	3181	775 064	31
Loma Pelada	3178	704 008	7, 31
Puntal de los Cuartos	3158	756 072	3, 28, 31
Pico del Tozal del Cartujo	3152	640 993	24, 31, 38
Pico del Cuervo	3144	746 057	3, 31
Puntal de Juntillas	3139	771 076	3, 28, 29, 31
Puntal de Vacares	3136	743 039	3, 28, 31
Pico de la Justicia o Atalaya	3135	753 063	3, 28, 31
Tajos Negros de Cobatillas	3116	761 076	3, 28, 31
Cerro del Mojón Alto	3107	742 063	31
Picón de Jérez	3090	773 082	28, 29, 31
Veta Grande	3085	686 019	23
Pico del Tajo de los Machos	3085	639 967	10, 31
Puntal del Goterón	3067	738 031	31
Puntal de las Calderetas	3066	741 035	31
Cerrillo Redondo	3055	635 964	10
Juego de Bolos	3019	714 019	23
Cerro del Caballo	3005	609 962	11, 12, 24, 31

APPENDIX B
Accommodation

Hostels

Albergue Universitario Sierra Nevada,
Hoya de la Mora (ski area)
tel +34 958 480 122
www.alberguesierranevada.com
reservas@alberguesierranevada.com

Camping

The following campsites are usually
open throughout the year and provide
cheaper alternative accommodation,
either in tents or cabins.

Balcón de Pitres
km51, Pitres, La Alpujarras
tel +34 958 76 61 11
or +34 958 76 61 12
www.balcondepitres.com

Órgiva Camping
main road south and just outside
of Órgiva
tel +34 958 78 43 07
www.descubrelaalpujarra.com

Camping Trevélez
Ctra Trevélez-Órgiva,
km32.5 18417 Trevélez
tel +34 958 85 87 35
www.campingtrevelez.net

Camping Las Lomas (Güéjar Sierra)
Ctra Güéjar Sierra,
km6.5 18160 Güéjar Sierra
tel +34 958 48 47 42
www.campinglaslomas.com/en/

Guarded refuges

Grid references in the following listings
relate to the Editorial Penibética map,
'Parque Nacional de Sierra Nevada'.

Refugio de Poqueira (2500m)
Grid reference 712 982
tel +34 958 34 33 49
or +34 958 06 41 11
www.refugiopoqueira.com
(live webcam)
refugiopoqueira@hotmail.com
84 beds (linen provided), meals
Open all year – booking essential

Refugio Postero Alto (1870m)
Grid reference 819 100
tel +34 616 50 60 83
or +34 958 06 61 10
www.refugioposteroalto.es
refugioposteroalto@hotmail.com
65 beds in seven dormitories (linen
provided), canteen and bar, hot water,
heating in all rooms, free WiFi
January to June: Wednesday 3.30pm
to Sunday 5pm; July and August: open
all the time; September to December:
weekends, holidays and festivals –
booking essential
Winter quarters open all year

Albergue Universitario de Granada
(2500m)
Grid reference 656 055
Tel +34 958 480 122
alberguesierranevada.com
reservas@alberguesierranevada.com

59 places (doubles and dormitories),
full meal service, open all year

Unguarded refuges

Refugio Horcajo (2220m)
Grid reference 786 030
Sleeping on concrete (or occasionally
an old spring mattress); water source
nearby (Barranco del Sabinar)

Refugio Vivac La Caldera (3100m)
Grid reference 710 010
Sleeps 16 on wooden boards; water
source nearby (Laguna de la Caldera)

Refugio Forestal Loma Pela,
Villavientos (3090m)
Grid reference 703 000
Sleeps 8 on wooden boards;
no water close by

Refugio Forestal Loma de Cañar,
Cebollar (2500m)
Grid reference 647 942
Sleeps up to 10 on concrete; water
source nearby (50m to the north)

Refugio de Ventura
Grid reference 587 929
Partially ruined

Refugio del Caballo (2860m)
Grid reference 611 965
Sleeps 8 on concrete; water source
nearby (Laguna de Caballo)

Refugio Elorrieta (3197m)
Grid reference 651 995
Three rooms with bunks; no water
close by

Refugio Vivac La Carihuela (3200m)
Grid reference 700 079
Sleeps 16 in wooden bunks; water
available (Laguna de Aguas Verdes)

Refugio Forestal La Cucaracha (1800m)
Grid reference 701 081
Sleeping on concrete or wooden
platforms; water 10min south west
(Fuente de los Lirios)

Refugio Peña Partida (2451m)
Grid reference 736 094
Sleeps approximately 10 on wooden
sleeping platforms; small natural spring
300m south east (Barranco de Peña
Partida)

Refugio Horcajo (2220m)
Grid reference 785 028
Sleeps 8 on concrete floors. Water from
nearby stream

APPENDIX C
Useful contacts

In case of accident or
emergency call **112**

Airlines

British Airways
www.britishairways.com

Easyjet
www.easyjet.com

Iberia
www.iberia.com

Jet2
www.jet2.com

Ryanair
www.ryanair.com

Weather

Agencia Estatal de Meteorología
(AEMET)
tel +34 807 17 03 65
www.aemet.es/en/

Teletiempo Sierra Nevada
tel +34 807 17 03 84

Sierra Nevada ski pages
www.sierranevada.es/en/
www.meteoexploration.com
www.eltiempo.es

Outdoor Equipment Shops

Walking/Trekking equipment and gas
cartridges can generally be purchased
from the following stores:

Decathalon, Deportes Sherpa, and Solo
Aventura in Granada

Deportes Nomadas in Durcal

Sierra Nevada Outdoor in Orgiva

Tourist Information Office in
Pampaniera

Information centres

Dornajo visitor centre
tel +34 958 34 06 25

Laujar visitor centre
tel +34 950 51 55 35

Pampaneira visitor centre
tel +34 958 76 31 27

Capileira visitor centre
tel +34 958 76 30 90
and +34 671 56 44 06

Administrative Center of the Sierra
Nevada National and Natural Park
tel +34 958 98 02 38

Protected Spaces of Andalucía
www.ventanadelvisitante.es

Spanish National Parks
www.spain.info/en/query/
spain-national-parks

Plants and wildlife

Waste Magazine
http://waste.ideal.es
An important and interesting online
resource that will help identify the
many varieties of species found in the
Sierra Nevada.

APPENDIX D
Glossary

Spanish	English
abierto	open
acequia	irrigation channel
agua	water
aguila	eagle
alberca	water tank
albergue	hostel
alcazaba/aljibe	fortress
alto, alta	high
aparcarmiento	car park
arenales	sands
arista	ridge
arroyo	watercourse
bajo, baja	low, lower
barranco	gorge, ravine
barrio	neighbourhood, district, suburb
borreguiles	high mountain grasslands
búho	owl
buitre	vulture
caballo	horse
cabra monteses	mountain goats, ibex
cadena	chain
calle	street
camino	path, track
campanario	bell tower
cañada	glen
cañuto	gully, corridor
carretera	road
carril	lane

Spanish	English
casa	house
cascada	waterfall
castaña	chestnut
cerrado	closed
cerro	hill
chorreas	waterfall
ciervo	deer
circunvalación	by-pass
collado	col, pass
cortijo	farm
cuerda	rope, ridge line
cueva	cave
cumbre	summit
derecha	right
descanso	rest
deshielo	thaw, de-icing
difícil	difficult
embalse	reservoir
ermita	hermitage
escalar	to climb
espolón	spur
este	east
estrecha	narrow
estrella	star
facil	easy
fiesta	festival
fuego	fire
fuente	spring, source
gota fría	literally 'cold drop' in weather terms
hielo	ice

Spanish	English
hoya	valley, basin
integral	whole, complete
invierno	winter
izquierda	left
laguna	lake
quebrantahueso	lammergeier (bearded vulture)
llano	flat
loma	shoulder, broad ridge
mirador	viewpoint
mochila	rucksack
mojón, mojones	cairn, cairns
molina	mill
montaña	mountain
mosca	fly
nevada	snowy, snowstorm
nieve	snow
norte	north
oeste	west
oruga	caterpillar
otuño	autumn
oveja	sheep
pared	wall
parque	park
paso	pass, way
pelado, pelao	bald
peligro	danger
peña	rock, boulder
peñón	crag
pico	peak
piedra	stone, rock
pozo	well
prado	meadow, pasture
primavera	spring

Spanish	English
puente	bridge
puerta	door, pass
púlpito	pulpit
punta	point, tip
racha	gust (wind)
rambla	watercourse (normally seasonally dry)
refugio	hut, shelter, refuge
río	river
romería	pilgrimage
seco	dry
sierra	saw (as in 'jagged mountain ridge')
silleta	saddle
sur, sud	south
tajos	steep cliffs
tiempo	weather, time
tubería	pipeline
vaca	cow
vasar	way, path
veleta	weather vane
ventisquero	snow patch, snowdrift
ventura	luck, fortune
verano	summer
vereda	path
veta	vein, seam
vía	way, route
vibora	viper
viento	wind
vivac	bivouac
yegua	mare
zorro	fox

APPENDIX E
Further reading

There are some wonderful books about the Sierra Nevada but, rather unsurprisingly, they are mainly in Spanish. The following, however, are particularly recommended.

Guidebooks

Visitor Guide Sierra Nevada (Organismo Autónomo Parques Nacionales)
A handy guide in English with chapters on geology, history, environment, ecosystems, access and some walking routes.

Sierras Andaluzas – Itinerarios Senderistas y Ascensiones, Manuel Gil Monreal and Enrique A. Marín Fernández (Editorial La Serranía)
70 itineraries covering not only the Sierra Nevada (of which there are 22) but also most other major mountain ranges in Andalucía.

Sierra Nevada – Guía de Montaña, Pablo Bueno Porcel
(Biblioteca de Bolsillo, Universidad de Granada)
Spanish guide to the Sierra Nevada including winter and summer mountaineering. Black and white photos.

Los Tresmiles de Sierra Nevada, Juan Luis Ortega and José Manuel Puela
(EUG Editorial Universidad de Granada)
Coffee table-sized book with superb photos and maps. Costly, but a really inspirational book for the winter fireside. A handy cut-down version of the larger book with black and white photos and maps is also available.

GR240

GR240 Sendero Sulayr, Sierra Nevada, Fernando Castellón de la Hoz
(Editorial Penibética)
Complete guide to the Sulayr GR240. Well written and can be understood with a minimum of Spanish. Concise details and clear maps.

Andalucía

Walking in Andalucía, Guy Hunter-Watts (Cicerone Press)
Guide to 36 graded walks in Andalucía, including Aracena, Grazalema, Los Alcornocales and Gaucin, La Axarquia, the Alpujarras and Cazorla.

Coastal Walks in Andalucía, Guy Hunter-Watts (Cicerone Press)
Guide to 40 coastal walks in Andalucía, including Níjar-Cabo de Gata, La Sierra de Mijas and La Sierra de las Nieves.

Images

Sierra Nevada en Images, Aurelio del Castillo Amaro and Antonio Castillo Rodríguez
  (Editorial Penibética)
  A fantastic selection of colour images collected from all seasons in the Sierra
  Nevada.

Sierra Nevada Parque Nacional, Roberto Travesí Ydáñez
  (Junta de Andalucía, Lunwerg Editores)
  A stunning collection of colour photos in a coffee table-sized book.

Plants, birds and animals

Las Aves de Sierra Nevada, Jorge Garzon Gutiérrez and Ignacio Henares Civantos
  (Junta de Andalucía, Sierra Nevada Parque Nacional)
  The book contains both Spanish and English translations. This is the ultimate
  guide to the birds of the Sierra Nevada. Wonderful photos and information; highly
  recommended.

Reptiles and Amphibians of Europe, E Nicholas Arnold and Denys W Ovenden
  (Princeton Field Guide)
  A really useful pocket-sized English guide giving lots of information to help identify
  and understand the reptiles and amphibians that you might encounter in the Sierra
  Nevada.

NOTES

NOTES

Mulhacén summit in mid-winter (Route 2)

DOWNLOAD THE ROUTES
IN GPX FORMAT

All the routes in this guide are available for download from:

www.cicerone.co.uk/917/GPX

as standard format GPX files. You should be able to load them into most online GPX systems and mobile devices, whether GPS or smartphone. You may need to convert the file into your preferred format using a conversion programme such as gpsvisualizer.com or one of the many other such websites and programmes.

When you follow this link, you will be asked for your email address and where you purchased the guidebook, and have the option to subscribe to the Cicerone e-newsletter.

www.cicerone.co.uk

LISTING OF CICERONE GUIDES

BRITISH ISLES CHALLENGES, COLLECTIONS AND ACTIVITIES

Cycling Land's End to John o' Groats
Great Walks on the England Coast Path
The Big Rounds
The Book of the Bivvy
The Book of the Bothy
The Mountains of England & Wales:
  Vol 1 Wales
  Vol 2 England
The National Trails
Walking The End to End Trail

SCOTLAND

Ben Nevis and Glen Coe
Cycle Touring in Northern Scotland
Cycling in the Hebrides
Great Mountain Days in Scotland
Mountain Biking in Southern and Central Scotland
Mountain Biking in West and North West Scotland
Not the West Highland Way Scotland
Scotland's Mountain Ridges
Scottish Wild Country Backpacking
Skye's Cuillin Ridge Traverse
The Borders Abbeys Way
The Great Glen Way
The Great Glen Way Map Booklet
The Hebridean Way
The Hebrides
The Isle of Mull
The Isle of Skye
The Skye Trail
The Southern Upland Way
The Speyside Way
The Speyside Way Map Booklet
The West Highland Way
The West Highland Way Map Booklet
Walking Ben Lawers, Rannoch and Atholl
Walking in the Cairngorms
Walking in the Pentland Hills
Walking in the Scottish Borders
Walking in the Southern Uplands
Walking in Torridon, Fisherfield, Fannichs and An Teallach
Walking Loch Lomond and the Trossachs
Walking on Arran
Walking on Harris and Lewis
Walking on Jura, Islay and Colonsay
Walking on Rum and the Small Isles
Walking on the Orkney and Shetland Isles
Walking on Uist and Barra

Walking the Cape Wrath Trail
Walking the Corbetts
  Vol 1 South of the Great Glen
  Vol 2 North of the Great Glen
Walking the Galloway Hills
Walking the Munros
  Vol 1 – Southern, Central and Western Highlands
  Vol 2 – Northern Highlands and the Cairngorms
Winter Climbs Ben Nevis and Glen Coe

NORTHERN ENGLAND ROUTES

Cycling the Reivers Route
Cycling the Way of the Roses
Hadrian's Cycleway
Hadrian's Wall Path
Hadrian's Wall Path Map Booklet
The C2C Cycle Route
The Coast to Coast Map Booklet
The Coast to Coast Walk
The Pennine Way
The Pennine Way Map Booklet
Walking the Dales Way
Walking the Dales Way Map Booklet

NORTH-EAST ENGLAND, YORKSHIRE DALES AND PENNINES

Cycling in the Yorkshire Dales
Great Mountain Days in the Pennines
Mountain Biking in the Yorkshire Dales
St Oswald's Way and St Cuthbert's Way
The Cleveland Way and the Yorkshire Wolds Way
The Cleveland Way Map Booklet
The North York Moors
The Reivers Way
Trail and Fell Running in the Yorkshire Dales
Walking in County Durham
Walking in Northumberland
Walking in the North Pennines
Walking in the Yorkshire Dales: North and East
Walking in the Yorkshire Dales: South and West

NORTH-WEST ENGLAND AND THE ISLE OF MAN

Cycling the Pennine Bridleway
Isle of Man Coastal Path
The Lancashire Cycleway
The Lune Valley and Howgills
Walking in Cumbria's Eden Valley
Walking in Lancashire

Walking in the Forest of Bowland and Pendle
Walking on the Isle of Man
Walking on the West Pennine Moors
Walks in Silverdale and Arnside

LAKE DISTRICT

Cycling in the Lake District
Great Mountain Days in the Lake District
Joss Naylor's Lakes, Meres and Waters of the Lake District
Lake District Winter Climbs
Lake District: High Level and Fell Walks
Lake District: Low Level and Lake Walks
Mountain Biking in the Lake District
Outdoor Adventures with Children – Lake District
Scrambles in the Lake District – North
Scrambles in the Lake District – South
Trail and Fell Running in the Lake District
Walking The Cumbria Way
Walking the Lake District Fells –
  Borrowdale
  Buttermere
  Coniston
  Keswick
  Langdale
  Mardale and the Far East
  Patterdale
  Wasdale
Walking the Tour of the Lake District

DERBYSHIRE, PEAK DISTRICT AND MIDLANDS

Cycling in the Peak District
Dark Peak Walks
Scrambles in the Dark Peak
Walking in Derbyshire
Walking in the Peak District – White Peak East
Walking in the Peak District – White Peak West

SOUTHERN ENGLAND

20 Classic Sportive Rides in South East England
20 Classic Sportive Rides in South West England
Cycling in the Cotswolds
Mountain Biking on the North Downs
Mountain Biking on the South Downs
Suffolk Coast and Heath Walks

CICERONE

Trust Cicerone to guide your next adventure,
wherever it may be around the world...

Discover guides for hiking, mountain walking, backpacking,
trekking, trail running, cycling and mountain biking, ski touring,
climbing and scrambling in Britain, Europe and worldwide.

Connect with Cicerone online and find inspiration.

- buy books and ebooks
- articles, advice and trip reports
- podcasts and live events
- GPX files and updates
- regular newsletter

cicerone.co.uk